I Don't
Remember
Getting *Old*

Margie Jenkins

OTHER BOOKS AND PRODUCTS BY
Margie Jenkins

You Only Die Once (Trade Paperback)
ISBN 9780996432009

My Personal Planner (Workbook)
ISBN 9780996432016

Don't Slam the Door on Your Way Out (CD)
ISBN 9780929488820

Don't Slam the Door on Your Way Out (DVD)
ISBN 97809292488813

I Don't
Remember
Getting *Old*

Margie Jenkins

PATIO PRESS PUBLISHING
Houston

I DON'T REMEMBER GETTING OLD
Copyright © 2020 by MARGIE JENKINS

More information on Margie Jenkins and her other books
is available at www.PatioPress.net

Many of the stories in I DON'T REMEMBER GETTING OLD
were printed in a little different format in the book, *You Only Die Once.*
This book is based strictly on my memories and may be remembered differently by others.

Library of Congress Cataloging-in-Publication Data

Jenkins, Margie.
I DON'T REMEMBER GETTING OLD Margie Jenkins
ISBN 9781671615106
1.Memoir, 2.Title, 3. Margie Jenkins, 4. Southgate, Kentucky, 5. Jenkins,
6. Four Generations of Stories, 7. From 1877 to 2020, 8. Life at Age 96, 9 Getting Old
10. From President Ulysses S. Grant to President Donald Trump.

Printed in the United States of America.
20 21 22 23 24 KDP 9 8 7 6 5 4 3 2 1

In memory of Jenks,
my husband of 70 years,
and
in honor of our fantastic children
Rick, Toby, Bob, and Susan

CONTENTS

ACKNOWLEDGMENTS

I am grateful to my amazing parents, who shared their stories with me about the late 1800s. My mother was born in 1877, the last year Ulysses Grant was president. My father was born in 1884.

I owe a debt of gratitude to my siblings, who taught me how to get along with others, to laugh at life and to make a difference in the world.

To Jenks, who fulfilled my dream to marry a tall, handsome man, have two boys and two girls and lots of puppies. To daughter, Susan, my computer genius, who retrieved the chapters I mistakenly deleted and worked with every page of this book.

To all four of our special kids and their families who have cared for Jenks and me and continue to be watchful of me, I am forever grateful.

To my writing consultants: Claudia Feldman and Doc Heatherley, who provided advice, love and humor as I struggled to tell my life stories. And to Bobby Sagmiller, who prepared this manuscript for publishing, I thank you all.

FOREWORD

hirty years after graduating from the University of Cincinnati, and being a stay-at-home mom while her husband, Jenks, built a very successful career in the oil industry, Margie Jenkins applied to enroll in the graduate school at the University of Houston. At first she was rejected on the grounds that she was too old and the graduate school had to save places for minority students and young people who could make a contribution. By her nature and character, not being one to give up easily, Margie persisted until the admissions counselor finally relented: "Well. Mrs. Jenkins, this next class does need a chronologically mature white female, and you might fit the bill." So, quoting Margie, she "became the token little old white lady in the graduate program of 1974." She earned her master's degree in social work at the age of 54. As a psychotherapist, she was employed as a marriage and family therapist at Houston' Interface Counseling Center and at the Memorial Drive Presbyterian Church.

At age of 60, Margie opened a private practice and counseled clients from age 9 to 90. At age 65 she became a newspaper columnist, writing a column called "Sixty-Something", addressing topics facing older adults. Many of her clients were facing end-of-life issues which, at the age of 79, led Margie to write and have published two of the most respected and widely read books on end-of-life planning— *You Only Die Once* and *My Personal Planner*.

When Margie and her husband, Jenks, were 88, they produced a DVD and CD called *Don't Slam the Door on Your Way Out* to motivate people to plan for life's final chapter.

They crisscrossed the country giving over 100 presentations about this difficult subject...in churches, universities, retirement centers, conferences, FBI groups, hospices...wherever they found an open door to help people plan for their own death and, much to their surprise, to enjoy the experience enormously. And then to discover that completing their end-of-life plans served up to them the freedom to live the remainder of their lives more bodaciously than they ever had expected.

At age 90, Margie became the creator and presenter of The You Only Die Once Course, a video study course offered to churches and various groups around the country. After retiring from her therapy practice at age 91, she became an entrepreneur and CEO of her own publishing company, Patio Press. We aren't sure, but it's likely she's the only 96-year-old publishing company CEO in the United States.

After Jenks died in 2016, Margie began writing her life story, titled, *I DON'T REMEMBER GETTING OLD*, the book you are now reading. As you read, you are meeting both the people who brought Margie into the world and who helped to shape her into the token little old white lady who was accepted into the University of Houston Graduate program 42 years ago—still going and motivating everyone her life touches to live bodaciously as long as they possibly can.

The Publisher

INTRODUCTION

*M*y life story spans almost a century. Add to that stories of my parents, and you have one century after another of remembrances.

To get ready to write about my life, I listed all the stories I wanted to include. When it reached 50 pages, my kids suggested, "Mom, you don't need to write about every memory you ever had."

My goal is to recall my 96 years of living—the ups and downs, mistakes and victories, lessons learned, and the love and joy that I felt from family and friends.

Each life is different, but some of my memories might coincide with yours. I hope you can review your life and celebrate, appreciate what others did to mold your life into the shape it became, and forgive yourself and others. Be kind to yourself.

I hope my life reflects God's love and adds a smile to those who read these words.

Happy reading.

Chapter 1

HULA DANCER

The year of my birth the world was still recovering from the effects of World War I. While jobs were scarce and hints of the impending Depression were worrying Americans, it wasn't all bad news. Jazz was big then and so were flappers, the Key Stone Cops and Charlie Chaplin.

I was born May 28, 1923, the fourth and last child of Mabel and Roy Little. They named me Helen Marjorie Little, but my siblings—Johnny, 9; Bobby, 8; and Francie, 5—called me the Shrimp or Shrimper. That was better than Helen, I thought.

A few months after I was born, President Warren Harding died unexpectedly, and Calvin Coolidge became the 30th president of the United States. It was said that Coolidge had a talent for effectively doing nothing, and he was known for the motto, "Eat it up, wear it out, make it do or do without."

Daddy lived by that adage also.

When a truck rolled down our street, loaded with watermelons, I rushed into the house asking for a quarter. After begging too many times, Daddy said, "Sit down. We don't have a quarter for a watermelon. You need to learn right now that there are always people who have more quarters then you have, and some have less. When we run out of quarters, we do without. Don't ask again."

In Southgate, Kentucky we lived in a butter-scotch-colored, two-story brick house, 24 steps up from the sidewalk on Linden Avenue. Johnny and Bobby slept in the back bedroom, and Francie and I shared a single bed in the alcove at the top of the steps. Mommy and Daddy occupied the front bedroom with two windows looking out across the street. They could see the olive, green mailbox where I mailed letters to Santa Claus. A white metal chamber pot with a handle and a lid was shoved under my parents' bed, a holdover from their childhood homes where they had no indoor plumbing.

Daddy remembered using old Sears Roebuck catalogs for toilet paper in the twohole outhouse. "Toilet paper is a luxury. Don't waste it," was a constant reminder.

On bath night, Daddy checked the amount of water I put in the tub. "You only need a few inches of water," he told me. When I was older, *after* he left the room, I locked the door and added more water.

A patch of fragrant lilies of the valley bloomed between our house and Grandpa, who lived in a small, shotgun-style cottage next door. I'd pick a bunch of the flowers to give to Mommy, remembering to cut the stems long enough to fit in a vase. She would sing a special song to me:

> White coral bells upon a slender stalk.
> Lilies of the valley deck our garden walk.
> Oh, how I wish that I could hear them ring.
> That will only happen when the fairies sing.

Today when I smell lilies of the valley and enjoy their delicious fragrance, I sing the song that Mommy sang to me. It gives me a warm, fuzzy feeling, waiting for the fairies to sing.

A narrow "crawl space" with a dirt floor under the front part of Grandpa's house was a secret hiding place for me. I snuggled into the dark, narrow space with my dolls and our yellow cat, Taffy. It had a cozy smell. I dressed Taffy in doll's clothes, and she became part of my doll family.

The crawl space was a favorite birthing place for Taffy. Being the only one who fit under the house, Johnny helped me wiggle through the narrow opening with a small basket to retrieve four newborn kittens, their eyes not yet open. Using a box and old towels, Bobby made a special bed for them on the back porch of our house.

Friends often referred to Daddy as a teacher. Some people even called him "Professor," but late each evening he left the house to work all night at the Newport Steel Mill. One morning on Daddy's way home he passed a band of gypsies who offered him a black puppy. He brought it home in his pocket. We called the pup Gyp, and he was my constant companion until our neighbor, Mr. Johnson, shot and killed him for getting into his garbage can. When Mr. Johnson walked past our house, I threw rocks at him, then hid behind a pillar on the front porch. Throwing rocks was not one of my skills so I never hit him, but I remember hating him.

On a cold, rainy night when I was almost 4, the sound of a man's voice woke me up. Wondering who was talking in the middle of the night, I stuck my feet into bunny slippers and sneaked out of bed. Feeling my way down the stairs in the dark, the voice got louder. My pink flannel nightgown swept against the steps while I held on to the wood railing. Reaching the bottom, I quietly opened the door into the living room and peeked around the corner. Sitting at the roll-top desk, wearing his faded brown bathrobe, Daddy held the phone receiver to his ear. Talking in a hoarse voice between coughing and sneezing, I heard him say, "I cannot come to work tonight." After a few minutes of silence, he repeated, "No, I won't be able to come to work. I have the flu and a bad cough. No, I can't work this week." His cough sounded deep like it was coming from his toes. After a long silence, he gasped, "Well, guess that means I quit." Hanging up the phone, he put his head on the desk and heaved a great sigh.

Something bad was happening. I was scared. Wanting to help, but not knowing how, I crept back up the stairs. Everyone was sleeping. Hoping Francie would waken to hear my story, I snuggled up to her. But she didn't move.

The next morning no one said a word about Daddy's phone conversation. Before Johnny, Bobby and Francie walked to school, Mommy filled their plates with tall stacks of buckwheat pancakes and hot brown sugar syrup. When I sat down for breakfast, Mommy made my pancakes in the shape of gingerbread boys. Daddy sat by the fire, smoking his pipe, still wearing his ugly bathrobe.

Later in the day, I sat on the kitchen table, covered with patterned oilcloth, watching Mommy peel potatoes for supper. Talking as she worked, she dropped peeled potato slices in cold water "to keep them from turning brown," she said. Cutting a thin slice of raw potato, she slipped it into my mouth. That was my treat. I loved hearing Mommy talk about things while she worked, even though I did not always understand.

She would tell me, "Put a clutch of posies on the dinner table to add a little color."

Or, "When you don't have much to eat, baking hot biscuits and honey make a better meal." Or, "Your father cared more about the teachers than he did his family."

What did that mean? I wondered. "I wish he was more considerate," she continued in a sad voice.

A dark cloud seemed to hover over Mommy and Daddy.

My brothers were always together, doing interesting things. Watching them was fun for me. Reaching into their pockets, they pulled out a variety of objects as they were needed: nails, pocket knives, golf balls, sticks of gum, skate keys, shiny glass marbles, ropes, a couple of pennies. Sometimes a hammer hung on their belts when they were building birdhouses or go-carts. Watching them added joy to my life. I wanted to do what they did.

Building go-carts was their project one summer day when I was 4. They hammered orange crates to boards and attached skate wheels to the bottom of the boards. Wanting to help, I reached over to touch the orange crate. Johnny pushed me away, "Get out of here, Shrimper. You're a pest."

After several failed attempts to get me to leave, Johnny banged me on the head with his hammer. Later, I was told the blow knocked me out. I collapsed as blood ran down my face.

Johnny rushed in the house screaming, "Mommy, I just killed the Shrimper."

A neighbor drove Mommy and me to the doctor, who told her the blow to my head did not seem to cause serious damage. But it might affect hair growth and leave a scar. That's how, at a young age, I developed a gray streak in my brown hair. Later at school kids called me "the skunk," and when I walked by, they'd sing, "The old gray mare, she ain't what she used to be." Cutting out the gray hairs with Mommy's sewing scissors did not prevent them from growing back. Covering them with black shoe polish didn't work, either.

Years later, when Johnny was in college, he sent me a hammer for my sixteenth birthday with a note, "Next time I'm home, Shrimper, you can get even with me and give me a gray streak."

Years later, working in Minneapolis, I was in a Walgreens drugstore when an elegant woman whispered to me, "What do you use to make the beautiful white streak in your hair?" I replied, "a hammer." She lost interest. But that is when I discovered my white streak was the envy of many people. Johnny had started a new hair trend.

In the backyard of our house in Southgate, an old, red henhouse provided chickens and eggs for family meals, until Mommy made Daddy tear it down because it was ugly and smelled bad.

Let me tell you about our backyard. Daddy created a big vegetable garden and each spring, he planted seeds and raised string beans, butter beans, peas, corn, carrots, radishes, asparagus and tomatoes. He spent most of his days working in the garden, planting, sprinkling, weeding and checking for bugs. Several fruit trees were scattered around the yard. Pear and apple trees grew near his garden, and a peach and a cherry tree were near his gooseberry bushes. A few grapevines gave us grapes for jelly. Daddy fed the chipmunks and the squirrels and tried to keep them out of his garden.

His vegetable garden and fruit trees kept Mommy in the hot kitchen all summer canning vegetables over the stove. I sat on a tall white stool and watched. Sometimes I held a big bowl of string beans and cut off the stems or shelled a mess of peas or butter beans as I watched Mommy make tomato relish, stewed tomatoes, and spiced peaches. My siblings and I climbed trees to pick pears and cherries. The cherries were sour and made me screw up my face when I ate one. But they made great cherry pies. In the kitchen was a special grinder that took the seeds out of cherries. I got to turn the handle, and it spits out the seeds and let the cherries fall into a bowl.

Mommy stirred the pots to keep beans and other stuff from burning. Steam filled the kitchen and fogged up the windows. The heat was unbearable. Mommy lined up mason jars on the kitchen table and filled them with all the things she cooked. When the jars cooled, she poured melted wax on top before she screwed on the brass lids. We kids had to take all the jars down the rickety stairs to basement cabinets. We would eat those delicacies in the months ahead.

After standing over the hot stove canning all day, Mommy had to take a nap.

While Mommy slept and Daddy worked in his garden, I decided to play store. The 15 steps upstairs made perfect shelves. I collected all of Mommy's pretty china dishes and glass goblets and placed them carefully on the steps. I arranged them according to color and size. The glass goblets were on a special step. Standing at the bottom of the steps, I admired my store. There was something pretty on every step. Then I got tired of the game and went outside to play.

When Mommy got up and tried to go down the steps, she had a problem. She had to remove my store items before she could get down the stairs.

When I came into the house, I expected Mommy would admire my display. Instead, I got scolded and told to help collect everything and put it back in the china cabinet. She reminded me to respect what belongs to others and not play with things that don't belong to me. That was my last time to play store on the steps.

One of my favorite things to do was to have tea parties with my dolls. I'd gather them together with my tea set and sit under the weeping willow tree, pretending we had cookies and tea.

On a hot summer day, Daddy was working in his garden, and I was the only one in the house. The doorbell rang and when I answered it, three, smiling, African-American women in long black dresses were standing there, collecting money for their church. I didn't have any money, but I invited them in. We sat in the living room. "You wait here," I told them, "and we will have a tea party." I gathered glasses of milk, graham crackers and napkins. We sat on the couch and had a tea party while we visited. One lady said, "This is the best tea party we ever had," and she patted my hand and said, "Thank you."

Before we had finished, Mommy came home. When

she saw me sitting on the couch with my new friends, she hustled them out the door. I complained, "Why were you so mean to them? They are really nice ladies."

Mommy said, "There is no such thing as a Negro lady."

"That's not true," I said. "I liked them. We were having a happy time."

That experience was the first time I realized that Mommy was prejudiced. I felt she was very wrong to treat them so rudely.

Some evenings, Daddy sat down on the piano bench and we four kids crowded next to him. He could not read notes but played by ear. We all thought he was a grand musician. We sang as he played the spirituals: *Way Down Upon the Sewanee River, Kentucky Babe, My Old Kentucky Home, Swing Low Sweet Chariot.* When we sang, *My Bonnie lies over the ocean; Bring back my Bonnie to me,* I cried because the words were so sad. It was only when I was older that I realized most of those beautiful songs were about slavery.

As a small child, I felt a dark cloud over our family, but it was never discussed.

One evening, after Mommy had gone to bed, Daddy and I shared a grapefruit at the breakfast table. "Doesn't Mommy like grapefruit?" I asked.

"Your mother doesn't seem to like much of anything these days," he answered.

"The Newport High School class of 1917 has invited your mother and me to a reunion dinner next month. But she said she will not attend. So I will go by myself."

"Why won't Mommy go with you?" I asked.

"Your mother won't go to any event at the high school.

She resents the teachers," he said. "Your mother always goes to bed before I do. She is not affectionate. She is kind of cold toward me."

"Maybe you should tell Mommy you love her," I suggested.

"When we got married I told her I loved her," he said. "If I change my mind, I'll let her know."

"That's not enough," I said. "Maybe if you helped her with the dishes she would be more loving."

"That's women's work," he said and stood up and left the room.

Doing marriage counseling at my young age wasn't working very well.

I had my own secret wish that I didn't share with anyone.

I hoped someone very important, like the King of England, would call and ask me to go around the world, maybe in a balloon, and somehow I would make everyone happy. We would play games, laugh, eat cookies and milk and love each other. But I didn't get that call, so I practiced on my family.

Trying to lighten the mood in our house, I planned "family nights." Invitations made out of red construction paper and stamped with Daddy's notary public machine were delivered to everyone: "Tonight meet in the living room for fun and games and treats." Everyone came, even my 90-year-old grandpa.

Sister Francie was a reluctant participant, but I talked her into singing with me. We sang and danced and played *Chopsticks* on the piano. Impressed with pictures of hula dancers in *National Geographic* magazine, I created my own grass skirt. I cut newspapers into strips, colored them green and looped them over my jump rope. Ole! I had a hula skirt and could hula dance. The family clapped and laughed.

For games, everyone had to line up at one end of the room and we played Captain, May I. Since I was the captain, they had to ask my permission to move forward to reach the other end of the room. Johnny with his long legs always won. When he asked, "Captain, may I?", I tried to slow him down by saying, "Take two butterfly twirls in place." On his tippy toes, with his hands over his head, he would twirl around and win anyway. We played Blind Man's Bluff and sang, "If you're happy and you know it, clap your hands." We ended family nights with a treasure hunt, hot cocoa and graham crackers.

My life goal at this point was to be a hula dancer and make everyone happy.

Many years later, Johnny, a Navy pilot stationed in Hawaii, sent me two real grass skirts with a note: "Don't ever stop hula dancing, Shrimper."

Chapter 2

LOLLIPOP FOR GRANDPA

Summer days were special when Bobby said, "Shrimper, make some peanut butter crackers, we'll hike to the woods, have a picnic and look for wildflowers." Holding a brown bag of crackers, we ran into the woods behind our house. Bobby showed me how to grab grapevines that hung from big trees. He pushed me, and I swung out over a little lake. When it was his turn, he ran fast, swung on the grapevine, and dropped in the water.

He knew where a fresh spring bubbled out of some rocks. We scooped up water in our hands and drank, and had our picnic surrounded by a field of white daisies. Sometimes he pulled a newspaper from his pocket and read me the Katzenjammer Kids comic strip. One day I picked up a rock nearby and a snake crawled out and slithered away. I screamed. Bobby said, "Don't scare the snake, Shrimper. You disturbed him taking a nap. He lives there."

Another special time with Bobby was when he said, "Shrimper, get a pillow, and we'll ride around Southgate on my bike." He put the pillow on the crossbar, lifted me up, and we rode all over town. I felt so proud to be riding around with my big brother. Sometimes we'd stop at Specht's drugstore and buy ice cream cones. Bobby taught me lots of things: how to roller skate, ride a bike, and play mumblety-peg. He could balance his pocketknife on his wrist or elbow and flip it to the ground, hoping to make it stick in the ground. I was never able to make the knife stick, but Bobby could.

He taught me to play Ping-Pong on Mommy's round dining room table, not the best place to learn.

On rainy days, sometimes Bobby made a circle with string on Mommy's carpet and showed me how to play marbles. That was after Mommy objected to his making circles on her rugs with chalk. He dumped a bunch of marbles from his leather marble bag into the circle and told me some of their names—agate, yellow jacket, and tiger's eye.

"Pick out a marble to use as your shooter and put it between your thumb and first finger. Try to shoot the marbles out of the circle," he said. He made a little bag for me to carry my own marbles.

Going blackberry picking with Daddy was an adventure, too. He put a belt around my waist and hung two buckets on it so I could use my hands to pick berries. When our buckets were full, we hiked home. Mommy had a pie shell ready and we'd have hot berry pie for dessert. Yum!

Francie liked to cook, and she showed me the marvels of cracking eggs to make cakes. When she made an angel food cake, she explained, "You can't let any of the yellow yolk get into the mix—you have to carefully separate it from the egg white." When I finally mastered that process, I knew I had become a real cook. Francie let me lick the pan when she made cakes or candy. But then she got a rubber spatula, scraped the bowl clean, and there was nothing left to lick. I hated that.

One day after making creamy chocolate fudge, Francie hid the candy in her desk drawer and locked it to keep Johnny from eating it all. When he discovered what she had done, he cut off the heads of her paper dolls. When I saw her headless dolls, I cried.

When I had a loose tooth, Johnny offered to help get it out. He tied a string around that tooth and tied the other end to the doorknob. He said, "Shrimper, you stand there away from the door, shut your eyes, and I'll count to three." Then he slammed the door and my tooth came out. It hurt and I cried. That was the last time I let him help me with a tooth.

Visiting Grandpa next door was a favorite excursion. He used a cane when he walked and had a mustache that he trimmed every day. Usually, he sat in a black leather rocking chair reading the Bible. On the table next to him he kept a narrow silver comb, a little pair of scissors and a wooden hairbrush. I combed and brushed his thin gray hair. Grandpa leaned back, shut his eyes and looked so contented.

One November day, I sat on his lap while we looked through his Montgomery Ward catalog. When we got to the toy section, we looked at dolls. "Which one do you like best, Little One?" he asked. Slowly he turned the pages, and I touched each doll with my fingers. There were baby dolls, Kewpie dolls, rag dolls, big dolls with hair of all colors. Some had blue eyes and others had brown. It was hard to think of choosing just one. But I finally picked a big doll with brown curly hair and blue eyes. She wore a pink dress with three pearl buttons at the neck and little white shoes. "Maybe Santa Claus will bring that doll to you," he smiled, folding down the page.

Under our Christmas tree that year were two big boxes. One was for me and one for Francie. She had chosen a Little Orphan Annie doll, but when she saw my beautiful doll, she wanted to trade. There was no way I would trade my doll.

Daddy thought it was wrong to cut down trees for Christmas. "That is a waste of trees," he explained. He bought a small live tree with a big ball of soil around the roots. We put it on a card table covered with red felt. The day after Christmas, Daddy planted the tree in our backyard. We ended up with a bunch of live Christmas trees in our yard. I wished for a tall Christmas tree that reached the ceiling, but that didn't happen.

Every day Grandpa came next door for meals, and on Wednesdays, he baked bread at our house. When I wanted to help, he looped a long white apron strap over my head and tied it around my waist. It hung to the floor. I sat on a tall, white stool and watched him mix flour and some other things in a big yellow bowl. Then he explained, "We need to add yeast dissolved in warm water to make the dough rise, then cover it with a tea towel and set it by the warm oven."

To watch the magic happen, I lifted the towel every few minutes. After a while, the dough had risen to the top of the yellow bowl. Grandpa reached in and punched down the dough and grabbed a handful to put it in my washed, floured hands. It felt soft and mushy. "You have to knead it gently to get out all the air bubbles, so the bread won't have holes in it," he explained. After watching him slap the dough from one hand to the other, I did that, too. Then we placed the dough into bread pans, brushed them with butter, covered them with the towel and let the individual loaves rise again. Sometimes we put a small lump of dough in my doll's bread pan. It took all morning to make bread.

While we waited for the bread to bake in the oven, Grandpa helped me set my dolls around the kitchen table ready for our tea party of warm bread and milk. The kitchen was perfumed with the scent of baking bread. Melted butter ran down my arms as I held the hot slice in my hands.

Grandpa died when he was 93. He was laid out in a casket in our living room. I kissed him goodnight before I went to bed. Friends and neighbors came to our house to visit Mommy and Daddy. They brought bouquets of purple iris, pink peonies, red roses from their gardens and plates of fried chicken, cookies, and chocolate cupcakes. My siblings and I got rowdy, and Mommy gave us each a lollipop to quiet us down. Mine was root beer, but Francie wanted it. She chased me around the house and outside. I ran in the house and hid my lollipop under Grampa's little white satin pillow in the casket. I knew it would be safe there. But the next day when they lowered Grandpa into the ground, I cried, "I want my lollipop." I explained to Mommy what I had done, and she said, "Oh, Grandpa will be so happy when he gets to heaven and finds his root beer lollipop." I wished I had put one in for Grandma, who had died years before.

I missed Grandpa. He was one of my playmates.

Early one Easter morning, Daddy called me outside. "I want to show you something special," he said. We walked to the front terrace and he pointed to a little spot in the grass. With a stick, he lifted off a ball of cotton. "It's a rabbit's nest," I squealed. On my hands and knees, I peered into the hole and saw three baby bunnies. "Oh, can I pick them up and take them to Sunday school? I'll be real careful with them."

"No", he said. "They are too young for us to touch them. They need to stay with their mommy. But I wanted you to see one of God's miracles that most people don't notice." He took my hand, and we walked into the house to get ready to catch the streetcar to go to church. I could barely wait to tell everyone in Sunday school about my Easter surprise.

Each Sunday morning Mommy browned a roast on the stove, then put it in a baking pan with peeled potatoes, carrots and onions. She covered it with a lid and shoved it in the oven to cook while we were at Sunday school and church. Daddy taught the men's Bible class, and Mommy was the president of the Women's Missionary Society. When we got home and opened the door, we inhaled that wonderful smell of Sunday dinner.

Election years were stressful at our house. Mommy was a strong Republican, and Daddy was a stronger Democrat.

In the primary department at church one Sunday, I sat on a little green chair and listened to a Bible story about the Publican and the sinner. At the dinner table, I told the family about the story and announced, "I know Mommy is a Publican so Daddy must be the sinner." Mommy agreed, but Daddy laughed.

Hanging on the wall in the Sunday school room was a colorful red and white banner with the letters J-0-Y lined up, one above the other. The teacher explained: "JOY results when you put Jesus first in your life, others are next, and Y is for yourself." I asked, "Why am I always last?" The Sunday school teacher said, "That's just the way it is."

After Grandpa died, I worried about other family members dying. I even gave God the idea that our house could burn down so we could all die together. Then I changed my mind. Burning the house down was not a good idea. I prayed that none of us would ever die.

For some reason, maybe someone told me, I thought God kept a little slip of paper for all of us, and when we'd do something bad, he put a mark on the paper. When the paper was full, we would die. To know when I would die, I got a little slip of paper and put a mark on it when I did something bad: I lied, did not do my chores or was mean to someone. My paper filled up—but I didn't die. Maybe God uses a bigger piece of paper, I thought, so I got a bigger piece, too. But that filled up also, and I didn't die. I guessed God uses a different system so I forgot about dying.

Making our family happy was my job so I just focused on that.

Chapter 3

CAMP COUNSELOR

The day after Labor Day in 1929 was special for me—the first day of school. Mommy made me a pretty red and white checked dress with a white collar and rickrack trim around the hem. I practiced wearing my new dress and shiny black Mary Jane shoes. Standing in front of the mirror I admired my new clothes. But I had to play in the house so they didn't get dirty.

When school finally started, Mommy hugged me and said, "You look pretty. Have a happy day." Francie held my hand as we walked out the front door and down the hill. Trying to be a big girl, I did not want to hold her hand. At the bottom of the hill, we had to cross busy Alexandria Pike, and Francie insisted I take her hand.

Miss Taylor, the first-grade teacher, had been teaching for many years so she knew Johnny, Bobby, Francie and my parents. A name tag was pinned on each new student. Mine read, "Helen Little." I crumbled it up and said, "I want to be called Margie. I need a new name tag." After some discussion, a new tag said "Margie Little." I felt more like a Margie than a Helen so I am glad I changed my name in first grade.

Several months later, Miss Taylor sent a note home saying, "Margie has trouble seeing the blackboard. I suggest you have her eyes checked to see if glasses would help." I heard Daddy say, "We don't have money for glasses. Margie just wants attention."

Later I learned that Grandpa paid for my glasses. Even though Daddy resented that, I got to ride the streetcar to Cincinnati with Mommy to see the eye doctor. A pretty lady with red hair helped the doctor test my eyes, and she gave me a penny because I did so well.

After several visits, I finally got my new wire-rimmed glasses. To celebrate, Mommy took me to Mills Cafeteria in the Dixie Terminal, where we would get a streetcar to ride home. She ordered cherry pie a la mode. It was the best thing I had ever tasted. On the way home, Mommy said, "Don't tell Daddy we stopped and got a treat. He will think it is a waste of money."

Glasses helped me see better and I enjoyed wearing them—until Mar Crites, a playmate, got mad at me for some reason and asked a shocking question. "Do you know you are adopted? You are the only kid in your family who wears glasses. That proves it. But if you tell your parents you know, they will send you back to the Good Shepherd Orphans Home on Grand Avenue."

I was devastated. Mar, two years older than I, was a pretty girl with long, black, curly hair and blue eyes. She wore cute clothes and made fun of the dresses Mommy made for me. Compared to Francie, who was beautiful, I thought of myself as kind of an ugly mutt as a kid with thick glasses and short brown hair with an ugly gray streak. I wished I looked like Mar or Francie. Afraid I'd be sent away, I didn't tell anyone. I cried a lot. When I finally told Mommy what my playmate had said, she was outraged. "Mar is mean-spirited. Don't play with her anymore. She is not a good friend." But I adored her and continued to be with her as much as I could.

Mar often came to our house to play, and sometimes we baked cookies. She suggested we sell them and make a lot of money. We put 10 cookies in a bag and walked around the neighborhood and sold them for 10 cents a bag. When we counted our money, Mar said, "Since I am older, I should get most of the money."

Again, Mommy was furious and suggested we make cookies at Mar's house. But her mommy did not want us in her kitchen. That ended our cookie venture.

I liked going to first grade. I met new kids. Mattie Morgan lived across town in a little house in the cemetery. Her father was the gravedigger. When I wanted to play with Mattie, I walked to Evergreen Cemetery and we played hide and seek among the tombstones. When her daddy dug a fresh grave, Mattie and I jumped in, stretched out at the bottom, held hands and played dead. Then we giggled and scrambled out. The cemetery was our playground.

At Christmas time, when everyone was talking about their Christmas trees, a boy named Milton said their family did not have a Christmas tree. When I got home, I asked Daddy, "Milton's family does not have a Christmas tree. Could we get his family a tree?" Daddy explained, "Margie, Milton is a Jewish boy, and they don't have Christmas trees. They have other celebrations. We need to respect their celebrations that are different from ours." I liked Milton and we roller-skated together.

On Valentine's Day in third grade, after all the valentines were passed out, the teacher found one last valentine at the bottom of the box. She lifted out a small red box and said, "It's for Margie."

"Who could be sending me such a fancy valentine?" I wondered. Carefully I opened the box and lifted out a chocolate heart from my sister, Francie. I couldn't stop smiling.

Mary Whitton sat next to me in class, and her desk was always messy. I helped her clean it out, and I told her, "It makes you smarter if you have a clean desk." Mary had long blond hair, but it looked like it was never washed. One day I took Mary Whitton home with me and washed her hair. Then I used my hairbrush to make it pretty.

A few days later my head began to itch. Mommy discovered I had head lice. She made me sit at a table covered with newspapers while she combed my hair with a very small toothed comb. It hurt a lot. She poured kerosene all over my head and then shampooed it. Mommy suggested I not bring Mary Whitton home anymore.

On weekends, Johnny and Bobby hitchhiked out Alexandria Pike to the Highland Country Club where they caddied for rich golfers and made lots of money. When they were in their early teens, they saved $15, enough to buy an old Model T Ford that didn't run. We did not have a garage so their Model T was parked in the street in front of our house, and my brothers worked on it day and night. When they finally got it to run, they taught me how to crank it to start. I felt so important. I'd sit between them, and we rode around Southgate. Gasoline was 9 cents a gallon. They drove to the top of Grand Avenue, turned off the motor to save gas, and we coasted down the hill really fast. My brothers were the envy of every kid in Southgate.

Late one night, Daddy heard a commotion outside; neighbor boys were trying to steal the Model T. Johnny and Bobby got their BB guns and ran out to chase the thieves. Our whole family went outside to watch the fiasco. The Model T had been pushed down the street, but the neighbor boys ran away to avoid the BBs. Soon my brothers got the car back in front of our house and safe.

About this time, a neighbor girl started flirting with my older brother. I didn't like that. I told Johnny, "Mae is not classy enough for you."

"Shrimper, what do you know about classy?" he asked.

I answered, "I just know she is not good enough for you." Johnny lost interest in her.

A few years later, a neighbor boy, Kenneth Petrie, and other kids came to my house to play "rock school" on the steps of our house. The leader held a rock in one hand and if you guessed which hand the rock was in, you got to move up one step. Kenneth liked me and always let me win. One day after Johnny had met him, he said, "Shrimper, that kid is OK to practice on, but he's not a keeper."

I lost interest in him.

When my brothers were in high school, they traded in the Model T Ford and bought an old Essex. They talked to Daddy about building a driveway so they could keep the Essex off the street.

Uncle Billy had lost his job in Cincinnati, and he and Aunt Ora moved into our home. After a while, they bought Grandpa's little cottage and moved next door. Uncle Billy liked to build things so Daddy talked to him about designing a driveway next to our house. All summer and weekends, Uncle Billy, Daddy, and my brothers dug a big hole with hand shovels in the terrace beside our house. It was hot and hard digging. I made lemonade and took it out to them. When they finished the big hole, they poured in cement. The driveway was very steep and narrow, but finally, they could drive the Essex up the driveway. It was years before Uncle Billy built a garage at the top of the driveway.

In third grade, fractions were a mystery to me. My grade was always low, and I felt bad about being so dumb. One evening Daddy said, "Margie, get an apple and let's learn fractions."

I wondered, "How could an apple have anything to do with fractions?" But it did. I sat on Daddy's lap and he held the apple and said we have one apple. He cut it in half and said now we have two halves of the apple. He cut the halves into two pieces and now we have four pieces called fourths. He wrote it down on a paper.

He suggested, "You eat one of the little pieces and how many fourths do we have left?"

I counted three-fourths were left. We each ate another piece of the apple; we had only one-fourth left. "Margie, you just learned about fractions." My grade in fractions improved.

Today when I eat an apple, that lesson in fractions still comes to mind.

In fifth grade, I became a Girl Scout. When it was time to sell Girl Scout cookies, my Scout troop went to Manyet's Bakery and watched Mr. Manyet bake the cookies. We counted out 12 and put them in white bags to sell in the neighborhood for 25 cents. For each bag we sold, we got a sticker in a book. If we filled up a book, we could go to

Scout camp free for a week. I was so eager to go camping that I sold enough cookies to go to camp for two weeks. The problem was other girls in my troop only stayed one week. I was alone the second week at camp and knew no one. I got homesick and cried. Bobby wrote to me, "Shrimper, you learn to swim, and I'll take you swimming in the Ohio River when you get home." That was motivation enough to get me swimming, and I enjoyed the second week of camp.

Soon after I got home, Bobby drove us down to the Ohio River. He knew a place where we could get in easily. I was excited but a little bit scared. He held my hand, and we stepped into the water. The Ohio River felt a lot different from the camp swimming pool. It was harder to swim. Suddenly, I got caught in an undercurrent that carried me swiftly downstream. I couldn't see Bobby, but I knew he was close by and a strong swimmer. He caught up and grabbed me, but the current took us both a long way from where we got in. Holding me, he was able to swim us back to shore. "You did good, Shrimper. You didn't panic when we got caught in the undercurrent." That was the only time I went swimming in the Ohio River.

One day I visited Jeanne Bloom, a Scout friend who lived across town. We pitched horseshoes in her backyard. I wasn't very good at the game. When I left to come home, she gave me a new puppy. Afraid my parents would not let me keep it, when I got home I hid it in Mommy's washing machine. Not a good place for a puppy.

The next morning, I had the job of cleaning out the washing machine. That was the last time he spent the night there. I made a special place for him by my bed, but mostly, he slept on my pillow. I named him Narmy because Johnny hung a Navy pennant above his bed while Bobby had an Army pennant over his. Narmy was a scavenger and prowled the neighborhood. He brought home fresh-caught fish from the Petries, who had left the fish on a table in their backyard. A box of butter ended up at our back door along with one rubber boot. Daddy made me give Narmy away to a farmer who lived out in the country.

Thinking back to camp, it seemed that the counselors had the most fun. They sang and danced, built campfires and made crafts. My new life goal was to be a camp counselor.

Chapter 4

ROAD TRIPS

In 1928 Grandma Little was very sick in Oregon, Illinois, and Daddy wanted to visit her. He and Johnny planned a trip to look at colleges in Illinois and visit Grandma. Going on a long trip sounded to me like an exciting adventure. I begged them to take me along. When they finally agreed, Mommy bought me a little red suitcase that I packed and unpacked many times with all my dolls and doll clothes. Francie bought me a multi-colored beaded purse and put in it a box of crayons, a coloring book, and a Tootsie Roll.

We left Southgate early in the morning. I was very excited and said goodbye to Mommy, Bobby and Francie. Daddy didn't know how to drive a car so Johnny drove us away from home in the old Essex the boys had bought. My stomach got in a knot when I realized Mommy wasn't going with us. We had not driven far when I discovered my new beaded purse was not with me. If I told them I forgot my beaded purse, I figured Johnny would get mad at me, he wouldn't want to drive home to get it and Daddy would yell at me for being forgetful and delaying their trip. Afraid to say anything, I started to cry. We were just about to drive across the toll bridge over the Ohio River to Cincinnati. Johnny said, "Shrimper if you are going to be a cry baby, you have to get out."

I sniffled, "I forgot my new beaded purse."

Johnny stopped the car. "Was he going to make me get out," I wondered.

"Well," he said, "we can't drive off without the beaded purse. We have to go back and get it." He turned the Essex around and drove back to Southgate.

After retrieving my purse, I got in the back seat with my dolls, my purse, and my Tootsie Roll, ready to have a fun time. I ate my candy and got out my coloring book and crayons. We drove for a long, long time.

I had to go to the bathroom but was afraid to tell them. I wet my pants.

The Tootsie Roll didn't last long. I got tired of coloring. *"Would we ever get to Grandma's house?"* It was not fun anymore, riding forever; I wished I had not come with them.

We stopped along the side of the road and ate the peanut butter sandwiches that Mommy had made us.

Finally, in the evening we arrived in Oregon at Grandma's white house with a big front porch. I was excited to visit Grandma. She and Grandpa Little came to Southgate when I was born, but I didn't remember that visit.

We walked up the steps into Grandma's house. It was dark and gloomy. The house was full of many sad and unhappy people I did not know. Everyone talked in a soft voice. I felt out of place and uncomfortable. Daddy talked to everyone, but no one talked to me. I was invisible. Grandma was in bed in a little dark room with a black curtain across the doorway. We tiptoed in to see her, but she was covered with blankets. I didn't know what to say. Someone said the word "cancer" and added, "Grandma is dying of cancer." We crept out of her room.

The next day we went to visit Aunt Sadie. She lived in a cheerful house with the sun shining in the windows. On the dining room table was a huge coconut cake. I walked around the table staring at the cake. Aunt Sadie asked, "Would you like a piece of cake?" How did she know? With a big butcher knife, she cut me a piece, put it on a pretty plate with a fork, and set it on the table with a glass of milk. It was the best cake I ever tasted. I am sure we had other meals while we were visiting in Oregon, but the big beautiful coconut cake is the only food I remember eating. There were no kids to play with, and I got lonesome. Everyone was old and looked sad. We visited other old relatives I didn't know.

Several days later, we left Oregon and drove to Jacksonville, where Johnny looked at Illinois College. We visited Mary Hyde Hall, a college friend of Mommy's, who invited us for lunch. Johnny was going to live with her while he attended college. We left for Southgate, and again it seemed like we drove forever before we got home. I felt like we had been gone a year. When we got home, I changed my big doll's name to Sadie.

Many years later, when I had a family of my own, our two daughters inherited my dolls. One day daughter Susan was playing with Sadie, and her older brother, Rick, was part of the action. I did not ever get the complete story but the result broke my heart. Rick told Susan that Sadie had been bad and needed to be punished. He

cut off her head and threw her in the closet. That action did not seem to bother Susan nearly as much as it bothered me.

Sixty-five years ago, when I discovered the headless Sadie in the dark closet, my thoughts flew back to my sister's paper dolls with their heads cut off by our older brother. But this event seemed even more tragic. I felt sick to my stomach and sat in the closet holding my favorite doll, tears streaming down my face. I must be a terrible mother. I doubted my parenting skills. What kind of kids was I raising?

I talked to Susan and Rick. They tried to explain it was just part of a game they were playing after watching a cartoon show on TV. I tried not to overreact.

They are just two little children playing a terrible game, acting out what they saw on TV.

Now at age 96 talking with my wonderful, loving and caring Susan and Rick about this story, they barely remember the event and are so surprised by my severe reaction.

I know kids often remember childhood memories differently, even when they grow up in the same family. I was always surprised by how differently my siblings remembered certain family events. Usually, no one could prove whose memory was correct.

Another surprise for me was how attached I still was to my Sadie doll. For better or worse, they didn't treasure the doll as I had.

Even though the country was suffering through a terrible depression, the 1933 World's Fair in Chicago was a hot topic in my family. My brothers had heard that Ford

Model A's would be racing at 50 miles-per-hour at the fair. A huge Ferris wheel was another big attraction. Then came this wonderful invitation from Daddy's Uncle Will Little and Aunt Letta. They wanted us to visit them in Chicago during the fair.

My brothers took turns driving the family to Illinois. On the way to Chicago, we stopped to visit Daddy's brother, Uncle Ralph, and Aunt Grace. They lived on the family farm near Oregon and had three kids; Dorothy was Johnny's age, Dick was my age, and Martha was younger. All the kids slept on mattresses on the front porch. In the barn, we jumped in the haystacks and played hide-and-seek in the cornfield. Having other kids to play with was fun.

Johnny spent most of the time with Dorothy while the rest of us petted the horses and cows and fed the pigs. One day Johnny drove Dorothy into town and for some reason, he asked me to go along. I sat in the back seat. We had barely left the farm when Dorothy reached over and kissed Johnny. I didn't like that. I thought about getting in the front seat between them, but they were too close together. Johnny and Dorothy were first cousins, and I didn't think they should be kissing. Maybe she was just one to practice on and was not a keeper.

My brothers did not date while they were in high school and later, I heard Johnny ask Dorothy, "When you go on a date with a girl, what do you do?" I did not hear her answer, but I can imagine what she told him.

The family plan was to spend a few days with Uncle Ralph, then drive to Chicago to visit Uncle Will and Aunt Letta and go to the fair. The morning we were ready to leave, there was a note on the breakfast table, but Johnny was nowhere in sight. The note read, "I'm staying on the farm. Go on without me. Johnny"

Mommy and I cried. Daddy said, "Stop crying and get in the car. We are leaving without Johnny." Bobby drove us to Uncle Will's house in Chicago. I thought I would never see my brother again. Daddy sat in the front seat. Mommy, Francie and I were in the back seat. It was a sad, quiet trip.

Uncle Will and Aunt Letta lived in a big building, and we had to ride an elevator up to the 10th floor to their fancy apartment. Uncle Will, Daddy's uncle, was a doctor with a mustache. Aunt Letta was a pretty lady with gray hair and a big smile. She hugged me. Uncle Will leaned down and patted me on the head. We sat around a table in a sunny room and had lunch.

After lunch, we sat in their living room, and I could see tall buildings all over Chicago. Uncle Will looked very serious and didn't smile much. As they talked, he reached up to the top shelf of his bookcase and pulled out a book and sat down. He called me to his chair and showed it to me. "This book is called *Tom Sawyer*. You should read it often, Merry Sunshine." I don't know why he called me Merry Sunshine, but he put the book in my lap and smiled. "You take it home with you and enjoy it." Since it was about a little boy, I was not much interested in it, but I thanked him and had Mommy read it to me.

The next day we all went to the fair. The only things I remember about it were a water fountain that turned on when you leaned over to get a drink and the Ferris wheel.

Bobby, Francie, and I sat in one seat for my very first ride. We went so high I could see the entire fair below us.

When it was time to leave Chicago, Aunt Letta fixed us

a snack to take with us, Daddy made a phone call, and we all got in the Essex. Daddy announced, "We are going back to the farm to pick up Johnny. I will go in and get him. Everyone else will stay in the car." We waited in silence until Daddy and Johnny walked out of the farmhouse with Uncle Ralph. Daddy shook his hand, he and Johnny got in the car, and we drove away. Our trip back to Kentucky was another quiet drive. I wanted to ask Johnny lots of questions like, "What did you and Dorothy do while we were gone?" And, "Didn't you want to see the fair?" And, "Did you want to stay on the farm forever and not live with us anymore?" But I was afraid to talk. Later that trip was always referred to as, "the time Johnny ran away." Mommy blamed Uncle Ralph, Aunt Grace, and cousin Dorothy.

In August, Johnny packed a cardboard suitcase, tied a rope around it and Bobby drove our family to the edge of Cincinnati. Johnny got out of the car with his suitcase, shook hands with Daddy and Bobby and hugged Mommy, Francie and me. I reached up and kissed Johnny. He smiled and said, "Where did you learn to kiss like that, Shrimper?" He walked to the highway and put out his thumb. He was going to hitch a ride to Illinois College in Jacksonville. We waited in our car until a truck stopped and Johnny got in. I cried, afraid I would never see him again.

Johnny had a plan – he was going to go to college and live with Mary Hyde Hall, Mommy's friend. She had offered Johnny a room and meals in her home in exchange for his shoveling snow, putting coal in the basement and other chores. Mary Hall's husband was old and dying, and she asked Johnny to help care for him.

Recently, I found a box of letters that Johnny had

written during his college days. The letters were in pencil on scraps of paper. He described living in the Hall home where a maid cooked the meals.

"No fried food is served so if I want fried eggs for breakfast, I have to get up before the cook. No coffee or tea is served because they are too strong, and they have long prayers before every meal. The weather gets down to 20 below zero and it is mighty cold shoveling snow. But I'm not complaining. They are very nice to me, and I appreciate their help with room and board. To make extra money, I shovel snow for five other families." He added a P.S., "Could you send some writing paper, a pen, and some stamps? And Shrimper, next time you make cookies, send me some."

Bobby was a senior in high school and had been given an appointment to the United States Military Academy at West Point by Daddy's friend, Sen. Brent Spence. That had been Bobby's goal since he was a young boy and read a book about Robert E. Lee attending West Point. Although Bobby was the valedictorian of his high school class, he failed the math section of the entrance exam and had to spend a year at the University of Cincinnati taking math courses. When he passed the exam, Daddy took Bobby to the bank so he could borrow $300 to buy his uniforms. That was the only expense at West Point. Daddy told him, "When you graduate, you will have to pay back the bank."

In 1935 our family got in the Essex and Bobby drove, heading to New York. We stopped overnight along the way at tourist homes. Back then, there was no such thing as a Motel 6 that kept their lights on for us. Notices along the highways advertised tourist homes that rented over-night rooms to travelers. Sometimes they also served breakfast but usually, it was just a room for one night. Daddy paid $3.50 for two rooms.

We also visited Mommy's relatives in Pennsylvania along the way. Grandpa had often talked about the "Ter-reberry girls" and Mommy wanted to stop and visit them. I was thrilled because I thought there would be girls I could play with. Somewhere in Pennsylvania, we pulled into a driveway next to an old brick house. We were greet-ed by two old women who hugged everyone. What a dis-appointment. The Terreberry girls were Grandpa's cous-ins and looked like grandmas.

When we drove to Weaversville, Pennsylvania, Mom-my's great uncle, David Weaver, invited us to a fancy hotel for a big family reunion and banquet. Johnny even hitchhiked from college to Weaversville for the event. The next day he hitchhiked back to college.

Bobby drove us to the town of West Point, New York, fifty miles north of New York City. The military academy was established in 1802. Bobby parked the Essex in a big parade ground, reached up to the baggage carrier on the roof of the car for his suitcase, and said, "I'll take it from here. You don't need to get out. You have a long trip back to Kentucky. Francie, guess you are the driver from now on."

We all did get out and kissed and hugged Bobby. Then Francie, age 16, drove us away from West Point.

I remember looking out the back window and see-ing my brother standing alone in the middle of a big area, wearing a brown cap and looking lonesome. My stomach was churning. It was hard to breathe. I was leaving behind a big part of my life, Bobby standing there by himself.

Bobby had taught Francie how to drive before we left on the trip. The only thing I remember about that drive home was Francie passed a car on a narrow road and got so close she took off both hub caps on the left side of the car she passed. Hub caps used to stick out from the wheels. She stopped. Francie and Daddy got out, picked up the hub caps from the side of the road, and talked to the people in the car. There was no other problem. We drove away.

In December of his first year at West Point, Bobby and the other cadets were encouraged to send checks to the charities of their choice and the academy would match them. Rev. Philip Vogel, the new young minister at our church, received Bobby's check for $300. He returned it to Bobby with a note saying, "Our church does not accept blood money from organizations that teach our young men to kill."

That rejection caused Bobby to lose faith in the church and to begin to doubt there was a God. I hated that minister for what he did.

When I was 13, I thought I was an unattractive little girl. But Bobby made a big difference in my self-image. The first time he came home on leave from West Point, one evening he said to me, "Shrimper, go get dressed up and let's go dancing at Moonlight Gardens at Coney Island." Francie was away from home, and I ran upstairs to look through her pretty clothes. I found a white linen dress that Mommy had made her with a bright green zipper down the front and green braid around the hem. I needed high heels to make it look right so I wore Francie's multi-colored sandals. When I came down the steps, Bobby said, "Shrimper, you look really spiffy."

Wearing his white dress uniform, he drove us to Coney Island, and we danced to Tommy Dorsey's orchestra. I felt so proud to be with my handsome cadet in his white uniform. I didn't know much about dancing but Bobby helped me learn. He treated me like a real date. I wished everyone I knew could see me dancing with my brother.

During Bobby's third year at West Pont, he invited us all to come up for "June Week." The car we had then was a Chevy Coupe, and it was too small to hold us all comfortably. Daddy decided to stay home, and Francie drove Mom and me to West Pont for the festivities. We stayed in a tourist home in the Pocono Mountains. Mom had made both of us special formals to attend the week's dances. Bobby's girlfriend, Skipper, was not available the first few nights so he invited me to be his date. I was 14.

Bobby got Francie a date with Harry Stella, a huge fellow football hero for Army, and filled out my Hop Card with the names of other cadets to dance with me throughout the evening. Bobby didn't tell anyone I was his little sister, and everyone treated me like a real grown-up. Dancing with the handsome cadets was thrilling, and they made me feel like I belonged. I fell in love with every one of them. All the other girls looked so sure of themselves.

After the dance, Francie had to drive us in the dark through the narrow mountain roads to our tourist home. Some nights the fog was so thick we could barely see the road.

Thanksgiving of Bobby's senior year at West Point he

sent us tickets to an Army/Penn State football game. We drove up to Pittsburg for the big game. Johnny had left college and joined the Naval Air Force, stationed in Pensacola. He got a weekend pass and rode a bus to Pennsylvania to see his brother play football. It was freezing cold in the stadium. Mom was so bundled up with blankets and overcoats that she almost rolled off the bleachers. It felt great to have the whole family together for a day and to celebrate Bobby playing football for Army.

During his senior year, Bobby wrote home, "Hitler is making noises in Germany and looks like he is going to take over Europe. Soon our country will be involved in that war. I will be better prepared as an officer, so I plan to sign up after graduation to stay in the Army. I hope to join the Army Air Corps."

Bob graduated from West Point in June 1939, and we all drove up to the graduation and watched President Franklin D. Roosevelt stand up and hand out the diplomas. I knew FDR was disabled by polio, but I did not realize how difficult standing must have been for him.

After graduation, Bob was stationed in San Antonio, Texas. In December of that year, he and Skipper were married in the West Point chapel. Fran and I were in the wedding. After the ceremony, the new bride and groom walked outside under the arched swords held high over their heads by his West Point classmates. It was just like my favorite movie, Flirtation Walk.

Chapter 5

MEETING JENKS

When I was in junior high school, earning my own money was a big deal. In seventh grade, I earned a quarter an evening babysitting for Fred and Fay Haas. They had a good marriage and a happy family, and they were my role models. Once a month they got all dressed up and went dancing or to the movies or out for dinner, and I stayed with their three kids. Sometimes we made peanut butter fudge, popcorn or cookies.

During baseball season, Fay and her friend Daisy Webster went to the Cincinnati Reds' afternoon baseball games, and she asked me to go with them so they could watch the game while I entertained the kids. Sometimes Fay asked me to take the kids to the movies to see *Snow White and the Seven Dwarfs* or some other kids' movies. When the Haas kids told their friends we were going to the movies, they all wanted to go. Sometimes I ended up taking nine little kids to the show on the streetcar to Newport.

When Daddy was elected treasurer of the Southgate School Board, his job was to calculate school taxes for homes in Southgate, deliver tax notices during the summer, and collect taxes before the end of the year. He asked if I wanted to earn two cents, the cost of the stamps, for each one I delivered. There were 2,500 houses in town. I could make big money.

I organized envelopes according to street addresses and stacked them in a shoebox. During the summer, I started out each morning with my shoebox of tax notices and delivered them around town. When the box was empty, I'd go home for a break, add another bunch of addressed envelopes to my shoebox, and go out again.

Each day I had to put on Daddy's roll-top desk a record of how many notices I delivered times two cents to show how much I earned. Daddy paid me once a week. It was a hot job but fun. I enjoyed getting acquainted with new parts of town. Sometimes I'd see friends who wanted to help. I gave them a stack of envelopes to deliver and told them, "If you do a good job, I will buy you a chocolate soda at Specht's drugstore." It was more fun having friends help.

Then I discovered they were throwing some of the envelopes down drain holes and not putting them in the right mailboxes. I bought them a soda one time, but told them I would have to deliver the notices myself to do it right. Other than babysitting, it was my first job of managing people.

I made the junior high basketball team, which was a great accomplishment. We played against other schools. I wasn't a star, but one evening I got home from a game and told Daddy I had made two baskets and we won. He said, "Margie, you are an athlete like your brothers."

The girls' team often watched the boys' games in the school gym. One night after their game, George Ashford, a tall, handsome ninth grader and the star of the team, asked if he could drive me home. That was pretty exciting. When we got to my house, we sat in the car and talked about the game. Then he reached over and kissed me and said, "Margie Little, I like you." I jumped out of the car and ran up the steps into the house.

The Southgate School Board voted to sponsor a school library. All the kids were given the opportunity to sell magazines to buy books. People who lived in the nearby suburb, called Fort Thomas, seemed to have more disposable income. I always went to that area to sell my magazines. I sold so many that I was named "Captain Manager." The first book I checked out of our new library was *Madame Curie*, but I don't remember what I read. I should read it again and see what it is about.

The summer after eighth grade Daddy heard about Camp Sunshine for underprivileged children and said, "Margie, maybe you could be a volunteer counselor at the camp." I spent four weeks there and had a wonderful time playing games with the kids and helping them make crafts. Sleeping in a cabin with six youngsters, sitting with them at meals, teaching them to swim, and acting out nursery rhymes made a fun, adventurous summer for me.

St. Teresa Catholic Church, located down the street from our house, built a roller-skating rink next to their chapel. A jukebox provided music, a Coke machine was handy, and neighborhood kids ended up at the skating rink every Thursday evening. Father Lehr, the priest, was always there, and sometimes he skated with us. That gathering spot was where I met Pat Fanning. We skated together and became good friends. He lived in nearby Fort Thomas but would sometimes walk to my house to visit. Pat helped me with Saturday chores, and we'd sit on the back porch swing and shell peas or stem gooseberries from Daddy's garden. One Saturday, I told Pat, "Today I am going to wash my hair so you have to leave."

He smiled and offered, "Margie, I can help wash your hair."

I leaned over the kitchen sink and Pat washed my hair, dried it and then combed it out. Mom did not like that.

Pat attended Highland High School in Fort Thomas, and I was in ninth grade, my last year at Southgate School. He invited me to several formal school dances. Mom made me a pink pique formal, and Pat came to the door all dressed up in a white coat and tie and black pants. He brought me a corsage to wear on my dress. He was the only one I knew at the dance, but it was exciting. The girls in Fort Thomas were more glamorous and sophisticated than my school friends. Later I learned the girls resented me for dating one of their favorite boys. I thought of Pat as a good friend, not a boyfriend.

When I finished ninth grade in Southgate, I had two secondary schools to choose from. Highland High in Fort Thomas seemed too fancy for me. I picked Newport High, where both brothers and my sister had gone.

Soon after school started in September 1938, I was sitting in Miss Phillip's history class next to a big talker, Dick Keitel, known as Kite. In the third week of class, Kite leaned over and said, "Bob Jenkins likes you."

"Who is Bob Jenkins?" I asked.

Not realizing that Keitel was a big jokester, he pointed to a mentally challenged boy on the front row. For several weeks I was especially friendly to that boy and smiled at him whenever we met. Then I discovered his name was Wayne Jones. One day Wayne said, "Margie, you are so nice to me. Are you my girlfriend?"

"I'm your friend, Wayne," I told him.

Soon, I discovered Bob Jenkins was in my Latin class. In early October, Miss Garvin, the teacher, suggested the class plan a picnic at Devoe Park in nearby Covington so we could get better acquainted. We were to bring hot dogs, buns, soda and the makings for s'mores.

A few days after the picnic was announced, a tall, cute guy stood waiting at the door as I walked out of class. He said, "Hi, I'm Jenks." I said, "Hi, I'm Margie."

He said, "I know. Would you want to go with me to the picnic on Friday?"

I said, "Sure." And he walked me to my next class.

He was athletic like my brothers, and he had a confident, sexy stroll that intrigued me. He wore a good-looking blue sweater and smelled like Old Spice after-shave lotion.

In history class the next day, Kite said, "Hey. I hear you met Bob Jenkins."

That's when I discovered "Jenks" was Bob Jenkins' nickname, and he and Kite played football together. Kite said, "Jenks is the best athlete on the team—maybe in the whole school."

The day of the picnic, I stood in my room deciding what to wear. I tried on every outfit in my closet. I wanted to make a perfect impression. Time was running out. I had to decide so I could catch the bus to school. After much deliberation, I put on my red letter sweater with a big "S" for Southgate. I wanted Jenks to know I was an athlete, also.

When I came downstairs, ready to leave, Dad said,

"Margie, why would you wear a Southgate sweater when you are attending a Newport event?" Of course, he was right. But I threw myself on the couch and cried. Mom comforted me and said, "Margie, you look wonderful. Everyone is going to love you." I dried my tears and ran to the bus stop.

Everyone in Latin class met at school and together we walked across the Eleventh Street Bridge. The toll was two cents, and Jenks paid for both of us. At Devoe Park, we roasted our hot dogs and sang songs. It was a fun evening, but several girls avoided me. Later I discovered that Jenks had dated them. I was an outsider, and they resented my dating their boyfriend. No one mentioned my Southgate sweater.

We all walked back to the high school and Jenks drove me home in his family's 1936 Oldsmobile. As we rode out to Southgate, Jenks yelled, "I see a 'bediddle.' "

"What's that? I asked.

Jenks explained, "If you see a car with only one head-light, and you yell 'bediddle,' you get to kiss your girl-friend." He stopped the car and kissed me.

Bediddle became one of my favorite words.

When we got to my house, we climbed the 24 steps to the front porch. He put his arms around me and kissed me. Seconds later, Daddy opened the door. I yelled at him to stop spying on me.

"You were leaning on the doorbell," he said. "I thought you were locked out." He shut the door.

That was October 1938, my first date with Bob Jenkins. I thought after kissing me he would call for another date. That didn't happen.

Later a group of girlfriends sat on my front steps talking about important things like who we would marry. I told them, "I am going to marry Bob Jenkins." They all laughed. "Why would you think that? He doesn't even like you. He hasn't called you since you had one date."

"I know", I said, "but that is what I plan to do someday."

Jenks avoided me for almost two years. He later told me he was shy, but I didn't buy that. He was seeing Jeanne Koenig, a glamorous girl who lived in his neighborhood. Our friend, Kite, told me decades later that Jenks and Jeanne had a flourishing relationship during that time. I even saw him and Kite at the perfume counter at Pogue's Department Store in Cincinnati that Christmas, buying a bottle of Channel No. 5. I knew it was not for me.

Kite told me that Jenks' mother did not want him dating Jeanne Koenig because she was Catholic. His mom's prejudices turned out to be a good thing for me.

Shortly after that one date with Jenks, a Southgate friend and I decided to sign up to play in an aerial dart tournament. It was played with a "birdie" made of a ball with feathers stuck in one end, and you batted it across a net with a wooden paddle. Bill Grimm and I beat all the competitors, and we won the tournament.

Not long after our big win, a group of girls and I were walking home from school when a car stopped. A guy leaned out the window and said, "Would you all like a ride?" It was Don Harrison, one of the senior aerial dart players that Bill and I had beaten to win the dart tournament. He drove all the other girls home before he took me home. Don asked me to go to the movies on Saturday night, and we dated until he graduated. I would have dropped him in a minute if Jenks had called. Don worked at Victor Brown's Florist and he often brought me big bunches of flowers.

Johnny had joined the Naval Air Force. One time when he was home on leave he saw the florist truck pull up in front of our house. He said, "It looks like Lover Boy is here again. He's getting to be a nuisance. Shrimper, he is OK to practice on but he's not a keeper."

Don graduated from high school and left for college. I did not date him after that.

In my junior year I dated Wally Winches, another cute senior, and we went to the prom together.

I was still waiting for Jenks to call.

Grandpa Martinis, age 92, 1935

Mabel Martinis 1898

Mabel & Roy 1915

Roy Little & Mabel Martinis, Wedding 1913

Johnny (L), Bobby (R) on bikes,
Francie fixing Margie's hair
and a neighbor, 1924

Bobby under a Model T Ford

Bob and Skipper at West Point, 1939

Francie, 9, and Margie, 4, with
her doll, Sadie and pup,
Gyp, 1927

Johnny a sophomore at
Illinois College, 1934

Johnny, Navy Pilot, 1937

Fran, American Airline
Stewardess, 1945

Navy Lt. Commander John Little
died in WW2, 1943

The Little Family:
Margie, Bob, Mabel, Roy,
Fran, John, 1939

Jenks, Newport High
School, 1940

Margie & Jenks
Eastern College, 1941

Margie & Jenks,
Wedding Day, 1946

Margie & Jenks,
front porch Steps, 1942

Margie & Jenks,
leaving for honeymoon, 1946

Jenks, completion of MBA at
Northwestern University,
1948

Margie, 1948

Unusual portrait
of Toby with her
daddy, 1950.

Jenks, baby Toby, Margie
and dog, Buck, 1949

Mabel & Roy Little, 50th
Anniversary, 1963

Margie & Jenks in the Alps, 1989

Chapter 6

STORY OF MY PARENTS
WHY WOULD A GIRL LIKE THAT MARRY YOU?

*M*y mother, Mabel Hope Martinis, was born in Knox, New York in 1877, the fourth child and only daughter of Rev. Alfred Martinis and Amanda Weaver Martinis.

The family moved often, whenever Mabel's father, a Lutheran minister, was called to start a new church. One of their early homes was in Hastings, Nebraska. In 1882 it was on the Western frontier, barely a settlement, with several dozen scattered residents, a meeting house and a one-room schoolhouse.

Unfortunately, there was no parsonage for the minister and his family. Reluctantly they moved into an abandoned shack with a dirt floor and no electricity or indoor plumbing.

To bring in extra income, my grandfather baked bread and sold it to neighbors in Hastings. Amanda, my grandmother, filled the pulpit on Sundays when her husband was unable to preach.

By the time my mother started high school, she and the family were living in Canton, Illinois. But her time in the public high school was short-lived.

In the first week of school, Mabel's teacher slapped her friend, Frank, across the face, and Mabel refused to return to school. Grandma Martinis home-schooled her in cooking, sewing, the Bible, literature, piano and organ, but felt she needed more education. At 16, Mabel received a scholarship to Carthage College Academy in Carthage, Illinois.

With a small suitcase packed with simple homemade clothes, Mabel rode the train to Carthage and moved into the school dormitory. There was neither running water nor heat in the building. During winter months, sometimes the basin of water she kept in her room turned to ice. Chamber pots under the bed served as toilets.

Mabel was an excellent student. When she finished high school, she was quickly accepted to Carthage College.

Mable's life changed dramatically in her second year of college.

Joseph Weaver, her wealthy uncle wrote to Mabel's mother to say his wife had died and his two daughters would be wearing black for a year of mourning. Could Mabel wear her cousin's clothes?

A trunk of beautiful clothes including lace-trimmed dresses arrived at Carthage College for Mabel to enjoy. Included in the trunk was a jewelry box full of lovely trinkets and a vintage cameo brooch.

The trunk was a wonderful gift. Mabel told her family. "I feel like a princess wearing these dresses. Seeing all these lovely things takes my breath away. I don't deserve them."

Mabel was the first woman to be elected president of the Cicero Literary Society on campus and the only woman to graduate in the class of 1897.

Later she became a buyer for a department store in

town, traveling to Chicago on business trips. She was self-supporting, unlike most women of her day.

My father, C. Roy Little, was born in Oregon, Illinois in 1884, the second youngest of a family of five. At 14 he quit school, thinking he'd learned all he could from books. It didn't take him long, however, to realize the mistake he'd made.

His mother took in boarders to help make ends meet, and they all sat around the kitchen table for meals. The conversation at one supper meal turned to marriage. One of the boarders, Miss Ida, a high school English teacher, asked Roy, "What kind of girl do you want to marry?"

Roy was quick with an answer. "The girl I marry will be beautiful, well-educated, musical, athletic, artistic, religious—an all-around wholesome girl who is fun to be with."

Miss Ida asked, "Why would a girl like that marry you?

"You dropped out of school and work at the piano factory, doing odd jobs. What kind of future could you offer a girl?"

That question changed Dad's life.

He shrugged, "No one in my family ever graduated from high school. It's too late now to change that even if I wanted to."

Miss Ida reminded the school dropout, "It is never too late to change for the better."

Quitting school was a dumb thing to do, he admitted, but he did not see a solution. Several years later, a Sunday school teacher suggested he think about completing high school at Carthage College Academy and said, "If you do well, maybe you could go to college." The idea of college sounded impossible. But he dared to hope.

Several years later, he applied to the academy and finished high school. One of his jobs was janitor of the Lutheran church on campus where my mother, who had already graduated, was the organist. While Roy cleaned the sanctuary, Mabel often practiced the organ. He noticed she was beautiful and musical. He fell in love with her music, but he did not know who she was.

By the time Roy entered Carthage College, he was older and more mature than his classmates. He was an excellent student and studied Greek, Latin and Hebrew. He could read the Bible in Greek. He was on the debate team and sang in the glee club. He joined the Cicero Literary Society and was elected treasurer. Checking the records of the literary society, he discovered several past students still had outstanding unpaid dues of $5. One of those owing money was Mabel Martinis. He visited her at the department store and discovered she was the beautiful church organist.

Mabel had noticed him walking across campus wearing a cap, his arms full of books. She paid her overdue bill and together, they began attending the young adults' group at church. At meetings, Mabel played the piano, and Roy led the singing. Church friends planned activities including hikes in the country, ice skating on the campus lakes and picnics in the park.

Dad later told me, "One special day, your mother and I rode our bikes out in the country to Baird Woods. We stretched out on a blanket and watched Halley's Comet, visible every 70 years. Halley's Comet will appear again in the 1980s. I won't be around then. But watch for it."

Sure enough, on March 13, 1986, two years after he died, a colorful Halley's Comet appeared on schedule. But like Dad, I won't be around when it appears again in the 2060s. So watch for it.

Mabel began attending Roy's glee club concerts, where he wore a tuxedo and looked very handsome.

When Roy was a college senior in 1910, he was chosen to teach English, the Bible and basketball at what was then known as the American University in Beirut, Syria.

As he prepared to leave, he thought about Mabel. Roy remembered Miss Ida, his mother's boarder, who had inspired him to reach for the stars. He thought, "Mabel fits all my criteria that I want in a wife—she's beautiful, musical, athletic, well-educated and fun to be with. Maybe a girl like that will marry me."

He was aware that Mabel was popular and had already had several marriage proposals. "I am going to be out of the county for three years," he thought, "When I return, she may not be available." He proposed to Mabel and asked her to wait for him to return from Syria in 1913.

There was no money for an engagement ring, but she agreed. She gave him a black and gray steamer blanket with his initials, C.R.L, embroidered in one corner. It kept him warm on his ocean voyage in a German ship.

Before Roy left on his journey, Dr. Hoover, president of Carthage College, asked Mabel if she would accept the position of dean of women. She was surprised and honored to be offered that opportunity, but she hated to leave her job as a buyer at the department store.

After much urging by the president, she accepted the offer. In 1910, both Roy and Mabel began new exciting new adventures.

As Roy sailed across the ocean, he could barely believe how his life had changed from being a school dropout and a "gofer" at the piano factory. He thought, "If only Miss Ida could see me now and know all the changes she inspired me to make."

Roy's hometown paper, *The Oregon Register*, asked him to send a monthly column about his Beirut experiences and the political situation in the area.

In his first column, Roy wrote, "Beirut is a beautiful city, often called the Paris of the East. My students range in age from 14 to 40 and are from Abyssinia (now Ethiopia), India, Egypt, Nigeria, Greece, Arabia, Turkey, Armenia and Bulgaria. Seventeen different languages are spoken here at the college. My job is to teach them English. What an amazing opportunity I have."

One letter that Mabel wrote to Roy said, "As dean of women, I am expected to teach social graces, etiquette, the Bible, and to act as a counselor to the girls. I feel inadequate to be teaching these things, but I am enjoying it. I have been asked to travel to several states including Missouri and Iowa to talk with potential students. This is an amazing opportunity for me. When I started college, I never dreamed I would have this kind of responsibility. I miss you, Roy.

Mabel"

Roy's letters to Mabel described his travels and college experiences. "I have three months of summer vacation and several long holidays during the year. A group of teachers travel around this part of the world. I swam in the Dead Sea. We have traveled by boat, train, donkey, camel, horse and buggy, and walked on the road to Damascus. I wish you could see these amazing places, Mabel.

Roy"

Toward the end of Roy's assignment, Mable received a letter saying, "My teaching job in Beirut ends June 1913. I am eager to get home to see you, but before I board the ship in England, I am going to stop along the way. I will send you picture postcards of places I visit."

Mabel kept a world map in her office at the college and stuck pins in places Roy visited on his way home. Multi-colored pins showed he traveled to Naples, Pompeii, Rome, Florence, Venice, Switzerland, Munich, Cologne and Liverpool, where he boarded a ship to Canada. She wished he would stop sightseeing and come home.

The young couple finally reunited at the Carthage College train station. Seeing her walk toward him took Roy's breath away. He had forgotten how beautiful she was. They kissed and hugged tightly before they went to the Carthage College lounge. Teachers and students had gathered there to welcome home the college celebrity. Everyone wanted to hear about his adventures. When Roy and Mabel were finally able to be alone, they talked about their wedding. It would be a simple affair at her parents' home.

But before they could marry, Roy had to have a job. Many schools and colleges sought him out as an experienced teacher and world traveler. He accepted a job at Mount Morris College, teaching world history, political science and the Bible among other subjects.

On Thanksgiving Day in 1913, my parents-to-be, Mabel Hope Martinis and Clarence Roy Little became husband and wife. Dr. Hoover, the college president, officiated. The newlyweds moved to Mount Morris, six miles from Oregon, and lived with Roy's cousins.

In January 1914 Mabel was offered a job teaching English at the Oregon high school and lived with Roy's parents. Roy's parents were different and less sophisticated than hers.

Most weekends, Roy walked the six miles from Mount Morris to Oregon to be with his bride. There was little privacy. It was a difficult year.

The following school year, Roy was offered an advanced position as assistant principal in the rough and tumble lumber town of Oconto, Wisconsin, not far from Green Bay. To prepare for his new position, he attended classes at the University of Wisconsin, working on a master's degree during the summer.

They rented the only house available in Oconto, and they were thrilled. Even if they did not have much furniture, they had a house of their own and privacy.

Logging was the main industry in Oconto, which was freezing cold from October to May. Most of the high school students came from logging families. They were a tough group, but Roy became their friend.

On a Saturday in May 1915, a group of students invited Roy to join them on a fishing trip across the Oconto River. Mabel was nine months pregnant with their first child and due to deliver any day, but she encouraged him to go and come home that evening. A violent storm kept the group overnight on the other side of the river.

The next day, Roy had to find a way to get home. He walked through the storm to a train station in Green Bay, took a train to Oconto, and got home late Sunday night. The next day, May 17, my older brother, John Risse Little, was born. Roy and Mabel were thrilled to start their family, and they loved baby Johnny.

During that summer, Roy registered for more postgraduate courses at the University of Wisconsin. He met W. P. King, superintendent of schools in Newport, Kentucky, just across the Ohio River from Cincinnati. King was impressed with Roy and encouraged him to apply for a teaching job at Newport High. The superintendent told Roy, "I plan to retire soon and will recommend you to become principal of the high school and be in line to become the next superintendent. You would be a great addition to the Newport school system."

Roy applied for the job and was hired as a history and civics teacher.

In August 1915 with high hopes and a promising future, Roy, Mabel and baby Johnny moved to an apartment on Maple Street in Newport, Kentucky. They were within walking distance of the First Presbyterian Church, where they became teachers and officers during their 60 years as members.

Roy was popular with students and teachers at the high school and the Newport school board. At the school, Roy helped organize a literary society, and he was in charge of the debate team.

The next year, Roy was named athletic director, and in November 1916 their second son, Robert Roy, joined the family. In December 1918 Frances Althea, their first daughter, was born. In 1919, Roy was named principal of Newport High. Life was good. Roy's future seemed secure. He and Mabel borrowed money from the Newport National Bank and bought their first and only home at 256 Linden Ave., Southgate, a small community about eight miles south of the school.

Roy was asked to speak about his Beirut experience at various churches and groups in surrounding areas. He was elected elder of the church and taught a men's Bible class that lasted 40 years. Mabel became involved with several women's groups, and she learned to cane chairs, hook rugs, make curtains and can vegetables. She was elected president of the Southgate PTA. Her flower gardens in the backyard were admired by all who came to visit.

The C. R. Little family was highly respected in the community. Hoping to complete his master's degree, Roy registered for more classes at the University of Cincinnati.

Little did they know that their bright future was about to come crashing down around them.

As I child I couldn't understand the tension between my parents. To me, they were such kind and loving people, yet they acted as though they were angry with each other much of the time.

I will try to explain what I discovered about the cause of their resentment toward each other. I did not know the source of the problem until Dad was 95 and leaving his old Kentucky home.

Chapter 7

GOOD-BYING PROCESS

On Easter morning in 1967, I called my 90-year-old mother in Kentucky to wish her Happy Easter. As soon as Mom answered the phone she said, "Oh Margie, wait a minute, I have some things I want to show you," and she left the phone. We were living in Kansas City then and had to watch our pennies. I was splurging a bit with a long-distant call.

I knew Dad would be sitting in his chair by the phone smoking his pipe. Since he was stone deaf, he could not visit on the phone.

After what seemed like an eon, Mom came back on the line and proceeded to tell me stories about some antique items she had kept in a box. She described a small, black, folding parasol that had belonged to my grandmother, Amanda Weaver. Her description of a beaded vest was so vivid I could visualize her mother wearing it to a special function in Weaversville. Also in the box were elbow-length lace gloves, a black velvet purse and a straw sewing basket full of colored darning yarn. Lovingly, she described a long, white christening gown and a small, child-sized, green pleated dress. She mentioned a homemade quilt with a red tulip design and a handwoven bedspread with the date 1821 embroidered in one corner.

These treasures were unfamiliar to me. Our phone

visit ended by each of us saying, "I love you. God bless you."

The next day Mom died.

When I got home to Kentucky, Dad showed me a box on the floor near the telephone marked, "Antiques for Margie." He said, "I don't know anything about these things but your mother seemed to enjoy telling you about them on the phone yesterday."

"Guess this is my inheritance," I said. Dad nodded. "Your mother left you much more than what's in that box, like her love for beauty, her trust in God, and her ability to be a good mother."

With awe and wonderment, I sorted through my new possessions. Did Mother know she was going to die? I don't know. But I know it was important for her to share her memories and stories while she was still able. Her treasures became invaluable gifts to my heart.

After Mom's memorial service, Dad said, "This has been a special celebration of a great mother, a loving wife, and an amazing woman. I wish she could have been here."

Then he smiled and said, "I guess she was."

Death ends life but not its meaning.

Dad continued to live alone in the house on Linden Avenue. I hired people to care for him, but he didn't want strangers in his home, and he fired them. To make sure he was doing OK, I went to Kentucky often to cook meals, mend his clothes and keep him company. I usually went alone, but sometimes Jenks would accompany me and make needed house repairs and help with the yard.

One morning, from the kitchen window, Dad and I

watched Jenks cutting grass, trimming hedges and raking leaves. He said, "Jenks is such a big help. He does so many things for me. I am amazed by what all he does." Then he turned to me and said, "Women do a lot of useless work."

I was stunned. I'm surprised I didn't knock him to the floor.

I pointed to a chair and said, "Sit down."

I felt so angry and disappointed in him I could barely contain myself. Since he could not hear my angry words, I had to write out my feelings. I wrote in big black letters, "I RESENT THAT. I come here six or seven times a year and do many things for you. I take you to visit your friends and invite them here for lunch. I make small meal-sized packages of food, identify them and put them in the freezer for you to eat after I leave. I wash and iron your clothes and clean your house. I don't think those are useless things."

Dad put his head in his hands and cried. With tears running down his wrinkled face, he said, "Margie, you're so right. And I never appreciated what your mother did for me. I am ashamed of myself."

I did not often get angry at him, but I felt I needed to stand up to him at that moment. My comments also made him realize how much Mom did for him, and he never appreciated her. I hugged him and wrote, "I forgive you, and Mom does, too."

For Dad's 95th birthday, Jenks and I went to Kentucky and created a happy celebration for him. Sister Fran came from California to join the festivities. I called the Kentucky Times Star, and they sent a reporter to interview Dad. The reporter asked Dad, "Have you lived in Kentucky all your life?" Dad answered, "No, not yet. I have lived in this house 65 years and I invite everyone to come here on May 10 and help me celebrate being 95."

Everyone turned out for his celebration—the police chief, the mayor of Southgate, the fire chief, the postman, the minister, neighbors, teachers, students, church friends. Old women struggled to climb up the 24 steps to our front door. Most of them came to me and said, "Your dad is a hero to us."

Or "Your dad saved my life. I can never thank him enough."

Or, "Your father sacrificed his job for us."

Or, "Your dad was a great teacher and a caring friend."

People brought candy, cigars, wine, joke books, large print books of short stories and poems, homemade cookies and blackberry pie. Kids who played checkers with Dad brought him a Hershey's bar.

After everyone left the party, I asked Dad, "What did those older women mean when they said those things about you being a hero, a special friend, and you saved their life?"

Dad took my hand and said, "Oh they were my students and other teachers at Newport High School when I was principal. They exaggerated. They are all good friends of mine. That was quite a celebration. Margie, you made a great party for everyone. I enjoyed seeing all those people. I felt loved and celebrated. Thanks to you and Jenks for celebrating my 95th birthday."

Three months later in 1979, Dad's neighbor called me, "Your father fell in the kitchen and knocked himself out.

We took him to the hospital, but no bones were broken, and he is OK. But we think you should come home."

When I got to Southgate, I found him sitting in his favorite chair looking depressed. I pulled up the old green leather footstool and took his hand. Since he could not hear me come in, he was surprised to see me.

He smiled and said, "Margie, I am glad you're here. I have been living alone since your mother died 12 years ago and I have done OK, but I need to leave my old Kentucky home. Find me a nursing home around here where I will be cared for and not worry you or the neighbors. I don't want to live with you in Texas or with your sister, Francie, in California."

I visited several nursing homes. I took Dad to see Carmel Manor in nearby Fort Thomas. After looking around and talking with the Mother Superior, Dad remarked, "This place is pretty fancy, but when can I move in?" We had to wait for a room to become available.

Dad and I had long talks about his life and possessions, trying to decide what he could take when he moved to his small room at Carmel Manor. His roll-top desk held many of his treasures. As we sorted through the desk, I discovered in the bottom drawer, crumpled, brown newspapers dated June 6, 1919, four years before I was born.

Ready to throw them out, I was stopped dead in my tracks by big black headlines, "**NEWPORT HIGH SCHOOL PRINCIPAL, C.R. LITTLE, TROUBLE MAKER, FIRED, BLACKBALLED FROM TEACHING IN KY.**"

I showed the article to Dad and asked, "What is this all about?"

He placed his pipe in the ashtray, patted my hand and shook his head in sadness. "That was a long time ago. I was the principal of Newport High and was told I was on the list to become the next superintendent. We had a bright future. But teachers, especially women, were poorly paid. They organized into a union and came to my office asking if I would go to the school board, represent them and ask for a raise. Teachers deserved more recognition and more money for the important service of educating our children. I agreed to support the teachers getting a raise.

"The school board meeting was held on a stormy night in a crowded room. I presented the teachers' union proposal and informed the board of their threat of going on strike. I supported the teachers. They deserved an increase in pay.

"Large groups of people who had heard that teachers' salaries would be discussed had pushed their way into the meeting. Thunder and lightning interrupted loud arguments and angry threats. Some stood on chairs to be heard. There were near fistfights between board members and people supporting the teachers.

"The meeting ended at midnight. The board voted to fire me, calling me a troublemaker, and they blackballed me from ever teaching in Kentucky again. That was a blow I did not expect. I walked in the rain to the streetcar station with a heavy heart."

I was stunned. "Aren't you angry about that?" I asked.

"No. I did what I thought was right, and the school board did what they thought was right. They voted to increase the teachers' pay so in one way, I achieved my goal. But telling your mother about their decision was the hardest thing I have ever had to do. Your mother never forgave me.

"The board's decision created a huge hardship for us, especially your mother. Jobs were hard to find. I worked the nightshift at the Newport Steel Mill for a while until I got sick and quit. I did substitute teaching in Cincinnati for a while and taught night school. But we never had enough money. We almost lost our home. Mabel's parents moved in with us and helped with the mortgage.

"I didn't handle the school board situation very well. I wished I had done it differently."

His hands trembled as he reached out to me. Tears filled his eyes. We sat in silence, holding hands, just being there for each other.

He looked at me, smiled and said, "But Margie, things warmed up between your mother and me, and as a result, you were born in 1923. We both agreed that you were one of our richest blessings."

At age 95, Dad was not only deaf, but he was almost blind. Before going to Carmel Manor, I wanted him to see his eye doctor, who was one of Dad's old students. The doctor discovered that Dad's good eye had a cataract that needed to be removed, but he could not do the operation for several weeks.

When we got home, I wrote to Dad and said, "We need to find a way to communicate because while you are in the hospital, you won't be able to hear or see."

Dad agreed. "I wondered about that. But I'll get along somehow."

In big letters I wrote, "We'll learn hand signals. When you are in the hospital and you ask me a question and the answer is YES, I will squeeze your hand once. If the answer is "NO, I will squeeze your hand twice. Let's try that with your eyes shut."

He asked, "Will you be with me in the hospital?" I squeezed his hand once. He said, "Yes."

He asked, "Will Jenks be there too?" I squeezed his hand twice. He said, "No. That works pretty good."

"Let's try palm printing," I suggested. He gave me a quizzical look.

"I will outline letters in the palm of your hand. Let's try it."

I printed out M-A-R-G-I-E in his palm. He laughed and said, "Margie." He wanted to try it in my hand so it became a game.

We were interrupted by a knock at the door. It was Bill Grimm, my childhood friend who was a roofer and had put a new roof on Dad's house. He and Dad had become great pals. Dad explained what we were doing—learning to communicate with palm printing.

Bill, a big jokester, wrote in big letters, "Get your eyes fixed, and I'll take you to see an X-rated movie." Dad laughed.

Carmel Manor called to say a room for Dad would be available in two weeks. When I told him, he said, "How do I leave this house after all these years and move into a room at Carmel Manor?"

"We'll have a 'good-bying' process," I told him and put my tape recorder on the kitchen table.

"What's that thing?" he asked.

I explained, "That is my tape recorder and I am going to write out questions and I will record your answers."

"Margie," he said, "you think of everything."

We sat at the kitchen table and I wrote, "Tell me about this table and the pie-safe in the corner. Where did they come from?"

Dad cleared his throat, sat up straight, his eyes came alive and in his loud teacher's voice he said, "This is like being on the radio. I've never been recorded before." He smiled and began talking about the things in the kitchen.

"My mother, your grandmother, Kate Fish Little, gave me this table when I married your mother in 1913. She took in boarders and we always had a lot of people sitting around this table. One of those boarders was Miss Ida, who changed my life when I was 14 and had quit school. She inspired me to go back to school and make something of my life. I have always been grateful for her wisdom. The pie-safe came from your mother's family, like these chairs that she learned to re-cane when the seats wore out. Your mother was a talented woman." Tears filled his eyes. "It's been 12 years since she died. I miss her. You and the neighbors have helped me live here alone. Your mother kept her bright-colored Fiesta Ware stacked in the pie-safe. Your daughter, Susan, wanted that. I'll miss this kitchen."

He nodded toward the window and said, "Each morning, I sit here, drink my coffee and watch the birds. Sometimes there are 10 different varieties at the feeder. They've come to depend on me year 'round. My grandpa, Isaac Fish, taught me to put a corn cob in the birdbath in the winter when it freezes so they can suck up the water through the cob. Usually, there's a family of rabbits in the yard somewhere. I haven't seen them lately. I enjoy watching God's creatures." A faraway look came to his eyes. "My animal friends will miss me. Time now for a nap."

A lot of good-bying awaited us, but we had started the process. In the days ahead, Dad and I sat in other rooms and talked about their contents. His yard was important to him so I knew we would walk around outside. And to the basement, where Dad remembered I hid my puppy in Mom's washing machine. We went to the garage as well as the attic —where he used to store the mummy hand he bought for 10 cents in Egypt. It was a prized possession. Everyone wanted it. Dad told me recently that he had given the prized mummy hand to my brother, Bob's children when they visited him one summer. "I have regretted that because they lost it," he told me.

Good thing we had two weeks to say goodbye to the house. I was glad I had brought several cassettes. Dad seemed to enjoy talking about his belongings and recording our conversations.

"I wish I could listen to the tape," he said. "I miss out on a lot of things not being able to hear. Can't hear the birds sing. But I don't hear babies cry and that's good. In my 95 years, I have heard a lot. Did you hear about the old-timer who got new hearing aids? He told his friend that he's hearing things that he never expected to hear in his lifetime. The friend said, 'Your family must be pleased.' The old man replied, 'Well, I haven't told them yet.' "

After naptime, we sat in the "front room" at his roll-top desk. I asked, "Where did you get this huge thing? It dominates the room."

The recorder recorded the constant tick-tock of the mantle clock that struck 3 o'clock.

He patted his desk lovingly. "I bought it for $5 from Proctor & Gamble in Cincinnati in 1921 when they modernized. It's been my office ever since. It has 19 drawers. Can you find the secret compartments?"

I explored the cubbyholes, each one filled with special memories. From one drawer Dad pulled out a gold watch. He held the old timepiece in his shaky hands and said, "My grandfather gave me this watch when I was 21. I'd like your son, Bob, to have it. He's about that age now."

A cigar box that served as the family "bank" was still in the top right-hand drawer. Among scattered coins in the bottom of the box was a scrap of paper. In a child's handwriting, the note read, "IOU 6 cents Margie."

"Guess you still owe the bank," he laughed.

In one drawer were pictures of Dad with a mustache, walking in the desert clutching a small Persian rug he purchased from peasants along the way. That threadbare rug was upstairs in the hallway. I was surprised at how handsome Dad was with a mustache.

"Your son, Rick, always wanted this roll-top desk. I hope he can have it," he told me.

Dad shuffled slowly to the living room where his old piano used to be. "Good thing you took the piano back to Kansas years ago. With my arthritic fingers, I couldn't play it anymore. I miss music. A lot of things have changed for me, but I don't remember getting old."

In the evenings, we sat together on the couch and looked at leather-bound books and old family photos that he could identify. One day we sat at the round dining room table and sipped lemonade while he talked about the furniture in the room. "That old cherry desk in the corner is the most valuable things we own. It came from your mother's family. Your daughter, Toby, always wanted it. Margie, you used to say, 'Why don't we get rid of all this old stuff and buy new things from Sears?' You didn't know much back then."

"What will you miss most in this room?" I asked.

Tears came. "Leaving this home is like tearing my heart out. I don't know if I can do it. I have lived here 65 years. The house is full of memories. I wanted to die here like your mother did."

For a few seconds, the only sounds recorded were the sobs we shared.

Together we walked to another room. Dad pointed to the old sewing machine. He said, "Your mother kept that machine humming, making clothes for you and Francie. After your brother, Bob, graduated from West Point, he left his heavy winter overcoat here. Your mother cut it up and, made you a gray suit with a jacket that had two rows of gold buttons down the front. It was one of her special accomplishments. You wore it to some fancy event at high school and were a big hit. I'll get my cane and let's walk outside." I put the strap of the recorder around my neck and we headed out.

"Your mother was in charge of the flowers, and I was in charge of growing vegetables. We were a good team. I have 43 trees in the yard. Some of them I planted from seeds. Some were our Christmas trees. When you were born, Margie, I planted that redbud tree. You both have grown and blossomed. When Amanda, your first grandchild was born, I planted the mimosa tree. You and Jenks planted all these dogwood trees for my birthdays through the years. I'll miss this yard."

To steady us both, I put my arm around his waist as we walked across the side yard. At the birdbath, he stopped. He poked around the tall grass with his cane and got down on his hands and knees. With a small stick, he removed a furry ball of cotton and said, "Looky here. Baby bunnies. Five of them, I think." I got down on my knees and could see little ears sticking out of the hole. "I've been looking for them," he said. "When I had a garden, the bunnies ate my lettuce leaves when they first came out of the ground. There won't be any lettuce for them this year."

By the end of the two weeks, baby bunnies skidoodled around the yard with the mother rabbit close by. We knew the time was near for Dad to leave. We sat close on the porch swing, "I wish Jenks were here," he mumbled softly. He reached for my hand and said, "It is hard to leave this place, but you helped me say goodbye to my treasures. These last few weeks have been some of the happiest times of my life, recalling all my memories. I had forgotten about some of those things. Now I am ready to leave."

I called Jenks in Houston and told him what Dad had said. Jenks was in an important meeting but said he would come to Kentucky as soon as he could.

Dad and I packed a small suitcase and planned to

leave the next day. He packed pictures of Mom and the family, his large print book of short stories and poems, the Bible and his book of crossword puzzles.

After living in the same house for 65 years, it is impossible to put your life in a bag and leave. We walked out the back door, the screen door banging behind us.

It was August 1979 when we drove down the driveway. Dad looked back. "Goodbye house. Goodbye birds. Goodbye trees and yard. Goodbye bunnies. This has been a good place for me to raise our family. I hope it will be a good place for you." Tears streamed down his cheeks. I was relieved he could not hear my sobs as we drove away from his old Kentucky home.

When we arrived at Carmel Manor, we went to his small room to get organized. Dad put his head on the desk and sobbed. Then he lifted his head and said, "That's enough. I will be well cared for here and won't be a burden to you."

Two weeks later, his cataract operation was scheduled. We arrived at the hospital, and he was put in a room and readied for the operation. I kissed him before they wheeled him away. In a short time, he was wheeled back to his room with patches on his eyes. His whole body was trembling, and he looked so fragile and helpless. I leaned over and kissed him, took his hand and made a big M in his palm.

He held my hand and said, "M, Margie is here. Everything will be alright." He relaxed and went to sleep.

Later that evening, our friend, Bill Grimm came to his room. He took Dad's hand and made a big X in his palm.

Dad laughed out loud and said, "Bill Grimm is here. You devil."

Dad recovered well and was able to read again. Jenks came to Kentucky and we invited Dad's friend, the minister's widow, to come for lunch back at Dad's house. That was the last time he would see his old home, but he walked around and seemed to enjoy seeing it again. After lunch, Dad surprised us when he said, "Well, I think I should be going home." Home was now Carmel Manor.

We sold Dad's house to a neighbor, and Jenks and I packed up everything that we could get in a big U-Haul truck and headed to Houston.

To give Dad something to look forward to, we told him I would come back in November, get him and fly us back to Houston for Thanksgiving with our family. He was excited about that.

On May 10, 1984, Jenks and I planned a birthday celebration for Dad's 100th birthday. His friends and special neighbors, Hilda and Irv Gries decorated a beautiful birthday cake for him and prepared punch and coffee. It was a fantastic event. Over 100 people came to celebrate with him. Our nephew made a video of the party, and Dad watched it over and over again as he marveled that "someone could make a movie of my life and 100th birthday celebration." Although he could not hear what people said about him, he could sense their love and admiration. As he watched the video, he smiled and cried.

The day after his birthday party, Dad took my hand and said, "Margie that was a great event. I felt loved and cared for. Thank you both for planning that party. I have had a great life for 100 years. Now I am ready to die. I can't see very well, can't hear, I have trouble walking and I hurt all over. You seem to be able to do everything, I want you to help me die and be out of my misery."

"God is not ready for you yet," I told him. "We have to think about plan B."

He looked me in the eye, "You're going to try to talk me out of dying, aren't you?"

I wished I could help him, but I did not know how to do that. I knew Dad was ready to die.

In October of that year, Jenks and I had planned a trip to Greece. The day before we were to leave, Sister Rose, the nun who cared for Dad at Carmel Manor, called me to say, "Your father has a serious cough and is not doing well. I think you should come home." I told her about our travel plans and asked her to tell Dad. Then I asked Sister Rose to put Dad on the phone to talk to me. He could not hear, but he could talk and express his views. With a very hoarse voice, Dad came on the phone and said, "Margie, I want you and Jenks to go to Greece, have a good time, bring me some Greek cigars, God be with you and I will wait for you to get home." Sister Rose said, "Well, Mrs. Margie, you have your father's marching orders. He will wait for you to get home. Have a safe trip and we will see you in two weeks."

Our trip to Greece was grand. When we got home, I called Sister Rose. "Please tell Dad we just got home. We had a great time. We brought him some Greek cigars. God was with us all the way. We will be in Kentucky tomorrow and look forward to seeing him."

Later in the day, Sister Rose called me. "Mrs. Margie, when I told your father what you said, he repeated it all. I had my arms around him and he said, 'Margie and Jenks are home. They brought me some Greek cigars.' And he died."

We all thought Dad was going to wait until we got to Carmel Manor before he died. Instead, when he heard Sister Rose tell him about our trip, he felt he had waited long enough. Dad had done what he said he would do— wait for us to get home.

When we got to Carmel Manor the next day, I went to his room and on the desk was an old envelope with his last requests written out on the back, "You and Jenks do my service here at Carmel Manor. Ask the nuns to play their guitars and sing."

Our kids came to Dad's memorial service, also many neighbors and people who loved him. The room was filled with Carmel Manor residents who had become his friends.

My father could not control all the events in his life, but he took control of his death.

Chapter 8

COURTSHIP AND MARRIAGE

My courtship with Jenks started off with a big bediddle kiss after the Latin Club picnic in 1938 but quickly cooled. I expected to hear from Jenks, but he pretty much avoided me. He said he was shy, but I didn't buy that. He was spending time with a gorgeous girl who lived down the street from him in Newport.

On Christmas Eve two years later, my girlfriend, Helen Meyer, called to ask if I would go to get a hamburger with her, her date, Gordy James and Bob Jenkins.

I said, "Sure."

I rushed upstairs to get dressed and when I came down, Dad said, "You're not going out at 9:30 at night on Christmas Eve."

"Oh yes I am," I replied.

Jenks came to the door, and after a quick introduction, we left for the Blue Star Drive-in in Covington.

After that, Jenks and I began seeing each other more regularly.

Several weeks later, on a beautiful snowy evening, we doubled-dated with Dick Keitel and Lelia Wright. When Jenks came to the door Dad asked, "Where are you going tonight?"

Jenks answered, "Me and Margie are going to a movie."

Dad, a grammar expert, said, "Margie and I are going to the movie."

Jenks laughed and said, "Hey, are you going, too?"

After that, Dad referred to Jenks as the "smart aleck." That moniker changed years later, but it took a while.

The four of us drove to the theater in Cincinnati, and afterwards we walked to Graeter's Sweet Shop for ice cream. As we were about to enter the shop, Kite sensed motion above his head and stuck out his hand. A bird pooped in his hand, and Jenks said, "Nice going, Keitel. Great reflexes!" We laughed so hard we could barely get in the door. Jenks kidded Kite about that for the rest of his life.

After our treat Kite drove us through the snow to my home in Southgate. When we got out, Kite said, "Jenkins, when you leave, you're on your own," and he drove away. The steps were slippery as we climbed up to the porch. When we got into the house, a dying fire welcomed us. We sat on the couch holding hands.

Jenks asked, "Margie, do you understand football? Most girls don't."

I said, "I know a few things but I'm no expert. Both my brothers played football at Newport High School."

"I heard about your brothers long before I heard about you," Jenks said. "Blue Foster, our coach, talks a lot about Bob Little and reminds us to be more determined, more aggressive and work harder like he did. Blue told our team that Bob Little was the best athlete he ever coached, and he played for Army when he went to West Point. And he was a fine gentleman."

Jenks grabbed a pencil and some scratch paper from the roll-top desk and began making O's and X's. "Let me show you some plays," he said. By the end of the evening, I learned more about football than I ever wanted to know.

It was after 1 a.m. when Jenks left my house, and I knew the buses had stopped running. The next day, he called.

"Last night, I had the most beautiful walk in the new snow in the moonlight," he said. "It was really cold, but I felt all warm after being with you. It was almost 2 when I got home, and the Sunday paper was on the porch. I didn't pick it up. Didn't want my folks to know how late I got home."

The next day Dad said, "I see you had a lesson in football last night."

As seniors, Jenks and I attended an evening award ceremony called "Class Night." Toward the end of the presentations, Jenks' name was called. He was wearing red pants, a bright yellow shirt, and a plaid sport coat. The auditorium erupted into a loud WOW as he walked across the stage. His face turned as red as his pants. He was named captain of the football team and given a medal and a small gold football.

The master of ceremonies then talked about the "N" ring given to the best all-around girl in the 1941 class of Newport High. I was shocked when he called my name. Receiving the coveted ring with a golden "N" on top of the black onyx setting was one of the most thrilling events of my life. The fact that Jenks and I were together that night made it even more special.

Recently, while cleaning out some files from Jenks' desk, I discovered a folder marked, "Personal." In pencil, he had written some notes, and one of them said, "Class night was great. Margie and I were together, and we each received memorable awards. But it never occurred to me that we would ever get married and be married for 70 years."

Guess guys don't think about stuff like that. But girls do.

We went to the senior prom together. It was held in the school gym, decorated like a southern plantation. We went with Gordy and Helen, and Mom made prom dresses for Helen and me. Since Mom made most of my clothes, I didn't realize how special that was, but Helen was amazed that Mom could make our dresses from pictures we showed her.

The prom ended at midnight, and we drove to Cincinnati to the Netherland Plaza Hotel to dance and share hamburgers and Cokes. I had never been to a hotel and when we walked into the lobby, it took my breath away. Gorgeous chandeliers hung from the ceiling, and walls were covered with photos of famous people who had stayed at the hotel: Winston Churchill, Franklin Roosevelt, Joe DiMaggio, Ted Williams and the 1940 Cincinnati Reds baseball team. That was the year they won the World Series.

As we walked toward the dance hall, we saw many other high school couples dressed in their prom clothes. At one end of the dance floor, we sat at round tables covered with white linen cloths. In the center of each table were elegant, silver salt and pepper shakers with "Netherland Plaza Hotel" engraved around the base. I took them home. I put them on the kitchen table, wanting everyone to know I had been to the fancy hotel.

The next morning, Dad woke me up at 6 a.m. and said, "Come downstairs."

He pointed to my beautiful souvenirs. "You stole these," he said. "They don't belong to you. I want you to write a letter of apology, wrap up the salt and pepper shakers and mail them back to the hotel. And don't ever steal anything again."

Lesson learned. I have not stolen much since then.

After graduation, Jenks received a four-year football scholarship to the University of Cincinnati. My father told me he did not have money to pay for college, but I could go to any school I could work my way through. That sounded great to me. I could go anywhere I could get a job. In retrospect, I wish I had broadened my college list, but I applied to the same school my sister had attended, Eastern Kentucky State Teachers' College in Richmond, Kentucky.

That fall I got a job as a receptionist at the women's dorm where I lived. It was a wonderful place to meet people—until the dean of women called me into her office in the middle of the year and told me I was fired. She would not give me a reason. I was devastated. If I didn't have a job, I would have to leave school. The librarian hired me to work nights. It didn't pay well, and sometimes I ran out of meal tickets. I ate a lot of peanut butter and jelly sandwiches.

Then I applied for and got the job as college postmaster. I had to get up at 4:30 a.m. to meet the mail delivery truck and throw mail into students' boxes. The hours were difficult, but I became one of the best-paid students on campus.

I didn't date at Eastern, but guys would often walk me home from my job or classes. Gail Roberts, an ROTC officer who played football, was kind to me, and when I invited Jenks to come to Eastern for the dances, he often stayed with Gail or some of the other football players.

Gail told me, "Margie, you have always acted like you are not interested in dating. Now we understand. You and Jenks look like you belong together."

Eastern was a good place for me. I made lots of friends, and it was exciting to have Jenks visit during special events.

On December 7, 1941, the fateful day the Japanese attacked Pearl Harbor, I was sitting with other students on the steps of the dorm when we heard the news. I rushed to a telephone and called home. Both of my brothers had been stationed in Hawaii at different times. I was relieved to hear Mom say that neither brother was anywhere near the Japanese massacre.

As a nation, we had been reluctant to join the fighting in Europe, where Hitler and the Nazis were slaughtering Jews. But this was a direct hit on Americans on American soil. Almost 2,400 servicemen and women lost their lives that day. Suddenly, we were a nation at war. All the men I knew wanted to fight the Japanese, and even I thought about quitting school and joining the war effort. I finally decided against it. Nevertheless, my life had changed. Even my relationship with Jenks was different.

That Valentine's Day was almost a deal-breaker for Jenks and me. Girls were receiving pretty valentines, flowers and candy in heart-shaped boxes. I received a box from Jenks. Friends gathered around me in my room while I opened it. Inside the box was a brown grocery bag containing a box of Ry Krisp crackers with a note saying, "I like my women skinny."

I was embarrassed and really angry at Jenks. Later he said it was supposed to be a joke, but it wasn't funny. During our 70 years of marriage, he often said, "Guess you're never going to forget that Valentine's Day."

He was right. I never did.

But later I realized that would have been something Johnny would do. Jenks and Johnny were both full of mischief.

My sophomore year at Eastern was unsettling, as if a heavy cloud hung over the school. A group of Army men arrived on campus for special training and took over one of the girls' dorms. We had to move. By then most of the men had left to join the war effort. I questioned whether I wanted to stay at Eastern.

In December 1942, Jenks called to tell me he was joining the Army and did not know what the future held. He and his football buddies were enlisting together. That was the last I heard from him for several months.

Later I learned the other nine guys, including Dick Keitel and Gordy James, passed the physicals and were sent to basic training. Jenks was rejected. The physical exam revealed he had a heart murmur and a hernia. He was handed a medical discharge and sent home. He would not talk about what that was like for him. I asked many times, but he would not discuss it.

After talking to my parents that summer, I decided to live at home and transfer to the University of Cincinnati.

Johnny had been sent to the South Pacific and his wife, Voris, lived with my parents while he was gone.

Both my brothers were officers in the service. Johnny was in the Naval Air Force and Bobby was in the Army Air Corps. Many years later I learned that Jenks was uncomfortable at our house, full of pictures of my brothers in uniform. He felt everyone thought he was a draft dodger. He hated that.

Jenks was 90-years-old before I heard the real story about his rejection. We were sitting on the back patio sipping wine and eating popcorn, enjoying the lake. I reached for his hand and asked, "Jenks, would you be willing to tell me more about your experience with the Army rejection?" He was silent for several minutes. He kind of chocked up. Very quietly, he began talking about what happened.

"That was one the worst times of my life," he said slowly. "I had played football with all those guys since junior high school. I was in sports all my life. I was shocked and embarrassed when I failed the physical exam. During World War II, everyone wanted to be in the service, everyone wanted to defend our country. I really hated it when my friends left for basic training, and I went home by myself with my medical discharge card in my pocket."

I reached for his hand and asked, "What did you do at home? Did you talk to your parents?"

"No", he said, "I didn't talk to anyone. I went to my room, shut the door and threw myself on the bed to think about my options. I had never felt so confused and defeated. Since I thought I was leaving school, I had goofed off and had not kept up with school work. It was final exam time and if I returned to school, I'd fail. Getting a job seemed the only solution. But I was not prepared to do anything. I had just changed majors from engineering to business. And the first thing they would ask would be my status with the Army. I lay on the bed for a long time with the door shut just thinking about what I could do."

We sat in silence. I could feel Jenks' hand trembling. Talking about this experience from more than 70 years ago was still traumatic.

Jenks squeezed my hand and said, "I didn't want to quit school and give up. I got off the bed and took a shower. Then I called my favorite professor at school, Dr. Ray Price, and told him my situation. He advised me to talk to my teachers and see what they would suggest. They were really helpful and gave me extra time to study for exams. Football had been canceled, but the school continued my scholarship so I graduated in 1945, same year you did, Margie."

Even though the war was over, Jenks was constantly reminded of his medical discharge.

"War experiences bonded men together whether at work or playing tennis. 'What branch of the service were you in?' 'Where were you stationed?' were common questions," Jenks said. "Being rejected from the Army caused me a lifetime of humiliation."

I said, "Thank you, Jenks, for telling me that long, painful story. It helps me understand many things about you, regarding our relationship and your thinking my father thought you were a draft dodger. At work, you were often questioned about your war experience, and even in your tennis group you felt left out of the conversations that were about war experiences."

In December 1943, our family was sitting around the fire in the living room. Dad was smoking his pipe, Mom was caning a chair seat, and Voris and I were in deep conversation. The doorbell rang which surprised us because it was late. The sheriff of Southgate, Syd Cornel, stood at the door. Dad and Syd were neighbors and friends. Dad suggested that the sheriff come in the house out of the cold. Syd stepped inside and said, "Roy, I have a telegram from the United States Naval Air Force. It could be bad news." He handed it to Dad. He opened the telegram that was outlined in black.

"The United States Navy regrets to inform you that Lieutenant Commander John R. Little is missing in action, December 28, in the South Pacific."

Mom, Voris and I began to cry. Father said, "Stop your crying. That won't help. Johnny is a survivor. He just might outlive this tragedy."

Mom, Voris and I went upstairs where we could cry without Dad scolding us.

Ironically, we continued to receive a few letters from Johnny that he had written weeks earlier. One letter was addressed to "The Shrimper." He asked me to send him a special dessert. He sent directions and drew diagrams of what it should look like. He began, "Buy a package of thin chocolate cookies, slap some whipped cream between them and line them up on a towel. Wrap them up and put them in the fridge overnight. The next day, spread a bunch of whipped cream over the whole thing. Then cut it on the diagonal (refer to diagram), wrap it in wax paper, put it in a box with some dry ice and mail it to me, U.S. Naval Air Force, USS Yorktown Aircraft Carrier, c/o Johnny Little, South Pacific. You better mark it 'Fragile.' I plan to feed that special dessert to my men at high tea and tell them my little sister, the Shrimper, sent it to me. Love, Johnny"

The letter made me cry, but I was impressed that in the middle of the war, he still had his sense of humor. After that, I hated everything Japanese. They had killed my brother.

Like most families, we had a radio where we could follow current events, but there was no such thing as television. Our family did not attend many movies, but after that telegram, we went more often. It was the only place we could see newsreels from the war, with actual footage of soldiers, hear gunfire, see blood and the hurt and pain on the faces of the men at war. Usually, the war news came on the screen at the end of the movie. That's when Mom would sit on the edge of her seat in the theater watching pictures of soldiers, sailors, and airmen scrambling around in the Pacific Islands. They were places we had never heard of—Okinawa, Solomon Islands, Iwo Jima, Guadalcanal, and Midway. She was sure she would see Johnny somewhere on the islands, and he would return home. But that was not to be.

A year later, my parents received another telegram stating that Johnny was assumed dead and that no trace of him or his plane was ever found. My parents held a memorial service at our church, which gave us some closure.

I was finding it difficult to be a transfer student at the University of Cincinnati. I knew few students on campus. Again I made an assumption that was incorrect. Since there was no football, I thought Jenks and I would see more of each other. I was wrong. We hardly ever dated. I would see him in the library surrounded by pretty girls. There were few men on campus so he was very popular. He said he did not date any of them, but he avoided me.

I joined a service group for girls on campus called the Cadet Corps, organized to be supportive of servicemen stationed in Cincinnati and in northern Kentucky. The sponsor was Dr. Helen Coops, my favorite professor. My senior year, I was named commanding officer of the Cadet Corps. Dr. Coops would often invite me to eat lunch in the faculty dining room while we planned activities. I became acquainted with officers at Fort Thomas who were interested in our group.

I was beginning to lose hope that Jenks and I would ever become a real couple. I wrote Jenks a note, "Jenks, although we have been dating for many years and we have had a lot of fun together, our relationship doesn't appear to be going anywhere. You seem to have lost interest in me, and I am ready to end our relationship and move on. Thanks for the memories, Margie." That was a sad day for me.

Jenks did not respond for several weeks. Later I learned that Kite yelled at him, "Jenkins, you talk about Margie all the time. You know you like her. Call her now and reconnect with her. If you don't, you'll be sorry."

After Kite's encouragement, Jenks did call and asked me to meet him in the library so we could talk. I was afraid to trust that things would be different, but we began dating again, and he was much more attentive.

Later he told me that my note to him felt like another rejection, but he realized that he really had not paid much attention to me, and he wanted to change that.

After we graduated from college, Jenks had a hernia operation, then went to North Carolina as director of a boy's summer camp near Lake Lure. I rode a train to Fryeburg, Maine, where I was a counselor at a camp for girls. Jenks and I exchanged a few letters. While I was at camp I applied for jobs at YWCAs around the country. I wanted a job by the end of the summer and hoped I could find a place where people came to have fun.

I got lots of offers and accepted the one from the Minneapolis YWCA on Nicolette Avenue. I had never been to Minneapolis, but the job included teaching a variety of things, and I liked that.

We were only home from our camp jobs for a week before I was preparing to leave. Dad said to me, "I don't have much hope for Jenks. He doesn't have a job and doesn't seem to be looking for one. I don't think he will ever amount to anything. You need to get rid of him."

With that thought in mind, I left on the train for Minneapolis. I didn't know if I would ever hear from Jenks again. I had mixed feelings – I was excited about my new job and sad that my relationship with Jenks seemed to be over.

The YWCA was an exciting place. I was teaching things that were new to me—like fencing, golf and square dancing. I also taught swimming to older women and disabled adults and cooking to foreign brides who wanted to learn

American ways. They were particularly interested in making hamburgers and chocolate chip cookies. On Saturday nights, the Y opened the swimming pool to Japanese men who were held in camps in the area. They were great swimmers, but they would try to get me in the pool by acting like they were drowning. I finally told them, "You guys swim better than I do so you are going to have to save each other."

I really enjoyed my coworkers, particularly a sweet young Japanese woman named Yoko Mizomoto. One day I had lunch with Yoko and confessed that I blamed all Japanese people for Johnny's death. I told her she was helping me get past that feeling.

She was very quiet for a moment, then said, "American soldiers killed my whole family but me." I was shocked. Of course, that is what war is about, but I had forgotten to think about that. Knowing Yoko was a healing experience for me, and I hope I helped her, too.

One weekend in the fall, two of my work friends and I decided we wanted to take a trip to Canada. But none of us had a car. When my brothers were teenagers, they hitchhiked from our house to a golf course in nearby Fort Thomas where they caddied. If they could hitchhike, so could we, I told the other girls.

We had one rule for safety's sake—all three of us had to agree to take the ride before anyone got in the car. That worked out well—except for one ride that was a little scary. We had waited a long time and it was getting dark when a car with three guys stopped. The girls and I looked at each other and decided to get in. Then we discovered they were drinking a lot of beer. After a short time, they drove off the highway to a dark park area. They encouraged us to get out and stretch and drink some beer with them. We got out and stretched, but we didn't drink beer. We told them we wanted to get back on the highway and go to Canada. They had other things in mind, but the three of us were strong and determined. It was late in the evening when we got to Fort William, Canada. We enjoyed our adventure. But we rode a bus back to Minneapolis.

In November, Jenks wrote me a letter. It was the most exciting mail I had ever received. He wrote that he was teaching business classes at William Wood College in Fulton, Missouri and would like to come to Minneapolis to have Thanksgiving with me.

WOW! I whooped and hollered and told everyone that my boyfriend, Jenks, was coming to see me. A woman friend at the Y offered to loan us a car for a day and told us about a little country inn that served a lovely Thanksgiving dinner.

I was renting a room from Mrs. Kelly and she offered her couch to Jenks so he would not have to pay for a hotel. We had a delightful Thanksgiving at the country inn. We returned the car and the next evening we rode the bus to St. Paul to go to a dance hall called The Prom. After dancing, smooching and talking, we were ready to leave. It was after midnight and we waited in the cold for the bus. I wore my new dress and high-heeled sandals that I had bought for the occasion and nearly froze to death. An old man ambling down the street said to us, "You're going have a long wait. Buses stop running at midnight." We finally got a cab back to Mrs. Kelly's house.

We sat on the couch and talked about many things. Jenks told me his professor, Ray Price, had recommended him for the job as head of the business department at William Woods. It was a girls' school, and he was having a great time. Then Jenks said, "I really missed you when you left. I didn't have a job, and I felt lost. Once I got hired at William Woods, I felt better about myself. I wished you were there with me."

Then I surprised myself and asked, "Jenks, are we ever going to get married?" He looked at me and said, "Margie, years ago, you said when you got married you were not going to work. On my salary, I can barely make it on my own. I can't afford to care for both of us."

"I'll work. I'll work." I said quickly.

"William Woods is looking for a health education teacher for next year. Would you be willing to apply for that job?" he asked.

"Of course," I replied. "I don't even remember saying I would not work when I got married. I like working. My mother did not work outside our home so I guess I assumed that's what happened when you got married."

Having Jenks spend Thanksgiving weekend with me in Minneapolis was fantastic for both of us. When he left on the bus to return to Fulton, I was sad but felt we had re-connected in a special way. I applied for the job in Fulton and the president of William Woods arranged to interview me at the train station in Indianapolis on my way home to Kentucky at Christmas break.

It was a stressful train ride from Minneapolis to Indianapolis. If I did not get the job, we couldn't get married. I got off the train at the station and met the administrator.

He was friendly and told me, "You have been highly recommended by one of our professors."

That was Jenks.

I got the job, and Jenks and I planned to get married August 21, 1946, in the little Presbyterian Church our family attended in Newport.

Yoko told me about her friend in St. Paul who made wedding dresses. After shopping for a long time I finally found satin material. Mother sent me the home-made lace from her wedding gown. Yoko's friend made me a beautiful wedding gown and charged $25.

My brother, Bob, came from California to be an usher. Fran was my maid of honor. Voris and Jenks' twin sister, Helen, were my bridesmaids.

We will never forget our first wedding night. Jenks had made reservations at the Henry Clay Hotel in Louisville. That was before credit cards. When we arrived at the hotel at 2 a.m., all rooms had been sold. Jenks said to the hotel clerk, "That's OK. Just call another hotel for a room for us."

The hotel agent said, "I'm very sorry but every room in the city has been sold out. The war is over, and the city is full of soldiers returning home. But you are welcome to sleep on the couch in the lobby, and here is a pillow you can use." We asked for another pillow, and then we stretched out at each end of the couch.

Later in the night, the hotel maid came by and asked us to lift our feet so she could vacuum.

The next day we rode a bus to Kirkville Lodge in Arkansas for our honeymoon. It rained the whole week. An older couple at the resort offered to teach us to play bridge. Jenks picked it up quickly; I was a slow learner. I hated bridge, Jenks and the rain. At the end of the week, the sun came out and we left. We rode a bus to Fulton, Missouri to William Woods College. Jenks had rented an apartment in what had been the Seminal Hotel. Classes had been delayed because the new girls' dorm had not been completed. We played house in our new digs and had fun, but we were low on money because we hadn't guessed that our paychecks would be a month late.

Part of our salary was the benefit of having meals at the college. Six girls sat together with a teacher at the head of each table. Jenks sat at the head of our table, and I was at the other end. Thursday evening dinners were formal affairs. Jenks and the few other men teachers wore tuxes, and students and the women teachers wore formal gowns. I had to be careful not to look like I was wearing a prom dress. After the formal meal, everyone walked to the chapel to listen to a music program or to watch the theater group perform.

At one formal dinner, I found myself trying to dig a cube of ice out of my iced tea glass. At the other end of the table, Jenks was shaking his head, indicating that sucking ice in that setting was not cool. I only did that once. But we laughed about it many times. During our dating, I was always trying to get Jenks to have better table manners. After one year at this fancy girls' college, he was correcting me.

Toward the end of the year, Jenks surprised me by saying, "If I am going to be teaching business classes, I need an MBA." He applied to several universities, and Northwestern accepted him. At the end of the school year at Fulton, we rode a bus to Chicago for Jenks to start his graduate program.

Apartments were impossible to find, but we were lucky to get a room to rent for $10 a week. We shared a bathroom and a kitchen with five other renters. I got a job at the Chicago YWCA and we both rode the L to our jobs. Jenks went to Evanston, and I went to downtown Chicago.

After one year, I lost my job at the Y. Since I was now the breadwinner in our family, I had to find a job quickly. I ended up selling World Book Encyclopedias to Polish immigrants in a poor area of west Chicago. It was a terrible job, and I was not good at sales. I felt these people needed to spend their money on other things rather than World Books—which is not a good sales pitch.

One cold week I trudged through the sleet and snow without selling a single set of books. On the last day of the week, I was wet, cold and discouraged when I walked into a warm restaurant and ordered hot chocolate. I put my head down on the table and cried. The very friendly owner came to me and asked if he could help. I told him my sad tale. He brought me another cup of hot chocolate and said, "There is no charge. Things will get better."

On the long bus ride home, I felt so grateful to that lovely man. He did not know how much his kindness lifted my spirits.

When Jenks graduated with his MBA, I was ready to celebrate. He had two job offers. One was with Standard Oil in Chicago, and one was with Continental Oil Company, (CONOCO) in Ponca City, Oklahoma. Jenks suggested we go to Kentucky and ask my dad for advice. That surprised me, but we rode the train to Kentucky, and Dad and Jenks settled in the living room. I listened but did not get involved in the discussion.

Dad asked Jenks about the pros and cons of each opportunity. Then Dad said, "Well, Jenks, you will be an asset wherever you go. I am very proud of what you have accomplished. You have been in Chicago for two years so you know your way around. You don't know much about Ponca City. What does Margie think is the best offer for you?"

Jenks laughed. "Margie has not had a very happy time in Chicago. I think she would prefer to leave. But she has told me that she would be happy to go wherever I think is the best opportunity."

Dad said, "Jenks, it looks to me like you have a choice between being a little fish in a big pond or a big fish in a little pond."

Jenks and I talked about the two offers, and finally, he chose Conoco.

The company paid to have our belongings shipped to Ponca City. Our total belongings consisted of four cardboard boxes, an ironing board, a card table and four chairs.

Chapter 9

CAREERS AND KIDS

"What do you want to be when you grow up?" That fifth-grade writing assignment resonated with me. Even at the tender age of 10, I'd already given this subject a lot of thought.

I wrote, "When I grow up, I will marry a tall, handsome man like my brothers, have two boys and two girls so everyone has a brother and a sister, but have them close together so they can all be friends. All the kids will have chores to do so that they will feel an important part of the family. I am going to live in a white house and have lots of puppies. My family will play together and have lots of fun, and everyone will love each other."

I kept in touch with the teacher who gave me that assignment, and many years later I sent her a photo showing our two boys and two girls with Jenks and me standing in front of our white house with our dog, Dana, and her 13 puppies. Mrs. Kendall wrote back, "Margie, you are one of the few students who knew what she wanted at age 10 and was successful in making it happen. Congratulations."

During most of my young years, I felt a lack of romantic love and consideration between my parents. In the family I planned to have one day, there would be more love shared between my husband and me. And our children would be closer in age.

Since Johnny and Bobby were so much older than I

was, I often felt like I missed out on having brothers. Instead, I had 3 fathers. Francie was five years older, and she, too, was like a parent.

Maybe it was my early interest in counseling. For whatever reason, I often tried to understand why my parents seemed so disappointed and distant with one another. As a kid, I played the role of fixer and entertainer. And I daydreamed about the man I wanted to marry and the children I hoped to have. In my dreams, we would be genuinely happy—no fixing required.

When I met Jenks at age 15, he didn't know he wanted to marry me. But I recognized him immediately. He was tall. He was handsome. He was intelligent and warm and funny, too. I knew we could be happy together.

Johnny was a jokester who added laughs and humor to my life—but he also had a mean streak that scared me sometimes. Luckily, he outgrew that. Bobby was my protector and playmate and included me in many of his activities. He also set goals for himself, and he was a dedicated student always striving to do his best. I wanted to be like Bobby.

Francie taught me how to cook and decorate cakes. From her, I learned to make peanut butter fudge, cupcakes and pull taffy. She was the beauty in our family and always looked pretty no matter what she wore. She was popular, too. She was prom queen in high school and voted "Miss Eastern" at college. After graduating from Eastern, Fran taught Home Economics at a high school in Pikeville, Kentucky and then became a stewardess for American Airlines for over 10 years before she married George and had two sons. She wanted the best for me and tried to teach me how to stand up tall, hold in my stomach and smile more. I thought she was bossy, and I did not follow her directions. I wish I had paid more attention to what she said.

I did what I told Mrs. Kendall I would do—I married a wonderful man and we created a happy loving family. But I had no career plans beyond that.

Jenks didn't have a plan for his life until he was teaching at William Woods and decided he wanted to get an MBA.

His MBA took us to Ponca City, a small, friendly town full of Conoco employees from all over the country. Our rented house on Peach Tree Street was owned and furnished by the local junk dealer in town. Jenks, a Market Analyst in the new market research department, could walk to work. Shortly after he started, the vice president of marketing invited all the new marketers to attend an orientation weekend at the Conoco ranch in Bandera, Texas. At one session, he asked each of the men what they hoped to accomplish for themselves and for Conoco. Jenks was the last one to answer the question and he said, "Someday, I want your job." Everyone laughed.

Twenty-five years later, after many moves around the country, Jenks was named Vice President of World-Wide Marketing. But in the beginning, we were just getting acquainted with our community. We joined the Presbyterian church in Ponca City along with many other Conoco employees and met the minister, Dr. Charlie Shedd, a huge, friendly man who became a life-long friend.

In Ponca City, we visited restaurants in town, but their food tasted odd to me. Even milk and orange juice didn't taste good. Jenks liked the Pioneer Grill, but I did not. That's when I discovered I was pregnant with our first child.

Charlie Shedd visited us and asked if we would organize a young couples group at the church. We started with 10 couples, but soon it doubled in size. We became known as the Sixty-Niners, a group for couples whose combined age was 69 or less.

That March my brother, Bob, called to ask if we could keep his German shepherd dog, Buck, while he was attending English War College in London. I agreed and told him I was pregnant. Bob said he would bring some baby furniture when he brought Buck in the next few weeks.

One day in April, I walked home from a church meeting and found baby furniture scattered around the driveway. And Buck, tied to the garage door, was trembling with fear. I sat down in the driveway and pulled Buck into my lap. I petted him, rocked him and whispered in his ear until he calmed down. He licked my face to say thank you. He bonded with me and the baby in my tummy.

Our little girl was born June 18, 1949, and we named her Linda Fran. "Linda" means beautiful and fit our baby well, and Fran was my beautiful sister who had provided me with maternity clothes and baby outfits.

But the name "Linda" did not last long. The first day of school there were six Linda's in her class. She changed her name as fast as she could and became "Toby." Most people don't remember we ever had a Linda.

In the hospital, Toby was a favorite in the nursery. Next to our baby with pink ribbons in her hair was Buffalo

Head, the 13-pound son of the Ponca Indian chief. Somewhere Toby has an almost twin Indian brother born at the same time in Ponca City.

I can't believe I did this but when Toby was just weeks old, I put her in the buggy, tied Buck to the handle and walked to town. I told Buck to "stay" and went into the grocery store to shop. When I came out, the baby was sound asleep, and Buck, guarding the buggy, was sitting exactly where I had left him. I put the groceries in the buggy, and we walked home.

When Toby was a few months old, we attended the Ponca Indian Reservation Dance Festival with another couple and their baby. Rudy New Moon and Charlie Chidbiddie were the dance stars. We later learned that both dancers had been important code senders for the Army during World War II. Enemies could not translate their Indian messages. They helped us win the war.

Our son Rick joined the family a year later. While Toby was an easy baby, Rick was more active and made his own rules.

Toby often says she feels she was born a grown-up; she had to take care of Rick when she was a year old.

Rick came home from kindergarten the first week and said, "One little boy had to sit in the corner all morning."

I asked, "What did you do, Rick?"

He explained, "Well, Jimmy pushed me first before I knocked him down."

Fortunately, Rick developed into a successful businessman and a loving son. He and his wife Dede became owners of one of the most successful real estate companies in Austin, and he calls every Friday evening to check on me.

Buck was an important member of our family for two short years. Then Bob, his wife, Skipper, and their three kids drove to Ponca City to reclaim their dog. Buck did not recognize Bob at first and stayed close to me. I could see disappointment in Bob's face and was relieved when a familiar gesture triggered Buck's memory, and he rushed to his old owner for joyous hugs and kisses. When they all got in their car and drove away, that was a sad day for me.

Jenks hugged me and said, "Margie, we will get our own German shepherd puppy someday."

And we did—when we were transferred to Houston a few years later. Dana Von Blitzen of Augsburg became our special dog who provided us with many litters of German shepherd puppies. We all loved her for 18 years.

It was 100 degrees when we moved to Houston in June 1952. We had no air conditioning in the car or in our rented house. The big event of the day was hearing the chimes from the ice cream truck. Each day I bought one popsicle that I split for Toby and Rick. They sat on the steps and enjoyed their treat. Rick wanted more treats, so he planted the popsicle sticks. The soil must not have been right for growing his crop. His popsicle sticks never sprouted.

Jenks was made Senior Market Analyst, and Conoco encouraged him to buy a house. They loaned us $13,000 for a home in Bellaire, Texas.

In 1953 Susan Beth joined our family in Houston. She was a mix of Rick and Toby with her tutu skirt, jeans and cowboy boots. She was a happy little girl with a mind of her own. Toby wanted to hold her and care for her. Susan would have none of it. She didn't want anyone telling her what to do.

Rick wanted a baby brother and in September 1955, our second son, Bob was born and completed our family. Rick was five and wanted his brother to do everything he did so Bob had lots of lessons in football and basketball before he could hardly walk. He was a willing student and tried to do it all.

Jenks felt he needed field experience if he wanted to advance in the company. He offered to take a cut in pay and asked for an opportunity to have a "line" job in the field as opposed to a "staff" job in an office. We were transferred to Minneapolis, and he was made City Manager. We waited in Houston for Bob to be born, and Jenks said, "We probably won't be back so let's name the baby Robert Houston." Later Bob said he was sure glad he was not born in Minneapolis.

We left Houston on a hot Thanksgiving Day in 1955 and drove to Minneapolis and were met with 20 degrees below zero. Jenks had rented a house on Park Road in Bloomington. Living in freezing weather with four kids was a challenge, but there were rewards, too. I sprinkled the empty lot next door every day until we had an ice rink. We bought used ice skates for everyone and learned to skate in the sub-zero temperatures. We'd warm up with hot cocoa in the house.

The best part of Jenks being a city manager was he seldom traveled away from home. He had a great boss and a good experience until he was transferred to Fort Worth in 1960 and became District Manager. Dana had her last litter of puppies, and I decided that was enough. Since we had given away my dad's piano, I wanted another one. I put an ad in the local paper that I would trade two German shepherd pups for a piano. It worked. Someone in a truck brought a used piano to our house and took two puppies. They got the best of the deal. Two piano keys did not play. I took group piano lessons and learned a little about playing by ear.

A year later, Jenks was transferred back to Houston and made Assistant Regional Manager. Instead of driving to our new house, we had to first take Jenks to the Houston airport for a long work assignment in England. The four kids, Dana and I moved into the house that was not quite finished. It was late October, and the house was chilly because there was no furnace yet. Houses were being built along our street, and many trees were cut down. I talked with a workman cutting those trees into logs. I asked, "Could I buy some of your logs to heat my house?"

"Can you drive a truck?" he asked.

"Yes," I answered.

He loaded a truck and said, "If you can drive this truck to your house, you can have the logs."

I went home to get 11-year-old Rick to help me, and he said, "I didn't know you could drive a truck, Mom."

"I didn't either," I answered.

We had been in our new house a month when Jenks' secretary called. She said, "Conoco is flying the company doctor to England, would you want to go along for a short visit with your husband?"

I said, "Sure, but I don't have a passport."

"Not to worry," she said. "We can get you a passport. Two other wives are going along. Be at the private airport at 6 a.m. on Thursday—that is Thanksgiving Day."

Where was I going to find a babysitter on short notice for four kids and a dog? I called Charlie Shedd, the Ponca City minister who had moved to a church in Houston, and explained my dilemma. He gave me the name of a church member who came to the house and agreed to stay while I was gone.

Somehow, I got myself to the airport on Thanksgiving morning. Conoco's small Gulf Stream plane needed to refuel often so our first stop was New York. After a quick Thanksgiving lunch in the grill at the airport we took off for Iceland.

We were the only people in the small Iceland airport. The dining room tables were decorated with flowers and candles, but they told us we could not eat there. They were expecting a large crowd.

A short time later, we heard lots of planes landing. Then dozens of uniformed Russian soldiers marched into the airport and filled the lounge. They came into the bookstore where I was looking around. They were huge guys, guns hanging from their belts, and they smelled really bad. I tried to be friendly but of course, they could not understand me, and I sure couldn't understand Russian. While I was trying to talk with these guys, the company doctor came into the bookstore and grabbed my arm. "Margie, I want you out of here. We don't need you to get kidnapped."

Later we discovered these soldiers were returning to Russia from Cuba after the missile crisis in 1961.

This trip was my first adventure overseas. I was excited but concerned about leaving the kids. We flew to Dublin and refueled again before flying to London.

When we finally made it to the Mayfair Hotel, my heart fluttered when Jenks came to meet me in the lobby. He looked so handsome and had been gone for a long time. I didn't want his hug to end. I felt safe and relieved to be in his arms.

The next day was Saturday, and Jenks, Bob Turvey and his wife, Marie, and I drove to a little village to see the sights. I don't really know where we went, but we ended up at the Red Lion Motel for the night. The clerk at the desk registered the Turveys and then looked at Jenks and me. She asked, "Do you have a marriage license to prove you are married?" That was a first.

I said, "No, but we have four kids in Texas. Does that count?" She let us stay in the motel.

The next day the guys went back to work, but I wanted to see London. I hailed a cab in front of the hotel and told the driver, "This is my first visit to London, and I may never get back here again. Would you show me the sights?" He smiled and we took off.

He showed me all the landmarks I had heard about, and in his beautiful English accent, he explained about the German bombing raids during the war and showed me many of the damaged buildings. We stopped at a tea house for a snack. When we got back to the hotel, I held out English money in my hand.

"I don't know your money so take what I owe you and your tip, and thank you for a delightful tour of your wonderful city."

He closed up the money in my hand and said, "Madam, it was my pleasure. There is no charge. Come again soon."

The next day London had one of its big, dense fogs. People on the street wore masks over their faces. The hotel got so foggy we could not see across the hall. The guys could not get to work. Jenks and I decided to go to a movie in the lower level of the hotel. The fog was so thick we could not see the screen.

The pilots left a message for the three wives to be at the airport the next morning. We got to the airport, but it was too foggy to fly. The pilots suggested we stay at the airport and when the fog lifted, we would leave. After waiting for several hours, we had to return to the hotel.

The next morning it was the same thing—too foggy to fly. Since I was supposed to be back in Houston the next day, I called home to tell the babysitter that we were fogged in. I said, "We hope to fly out tomorrow, but we might be fogged in again. Do you think you can hang in there for a couple more days?" There was a long silence. I could tell things had not been great for her or the kids. She replied, "Well, I guess."

The next day we tried again. The fog was still heavy. The pilots said, "Stick around."

Soon they announced, "Board the plane. We're leaving."

We did, but I could hear the pilots talking to each other. "Can you see the yellow line?" The answer was NO. Later I heard the question again. The answer was, "A little better, but no."

A few minutes later, the pilot said, "OK. Let's go."

Within minutes we were above the clouds and fog, and we were flying in bright sunshine. We had a pleasant flight back to Houston.

The kids were really glad to see me; the sitter was really glad to leave. It had been a tough week for everyone.

In 1963, Fran and I decided to have a 50th wedding anniversary party in Houston for our parents. Fran made a beautiful wedding cake. Our parents were surrounded by kids and grandkids. The celebration was a happy occasion for everyone. Jenks wrote out a script, "This is your Life," and gave Dad a copy so he could read what Jenks was saying as he showed pictures on a screen. Photos included Dad riding a camel in Egypt, scenes from his years in Beirut, and my mother as dean of women at Carthage College. Friends and relatives from around the world sent cards and small gifts. It seemed that the gathering of the family and all the attention from friends made my parents happy and relaxed. I was so pleased to see them being especially loving to each other.

That gathering was the last time our family was together.

In 1964 Jenks was promoted to Regional Manager and transferred to Kansas City. Toby was chosen to be an exchange student to Cairo, Egypt when she was a junior in high school. While the language, food, and culture took a lot of getting used to, she had a fantastic experience and came home speaking Arabic. We invited Mom and Dad to come to Kansas City for Thanksgiving to hear Toby report on her journey. She and Dad had fun comparing Egypt in 1910 and 1966.

In 1967, I called Mom to wish her a happy Easter.

The next day, she died. We all went back to Kentucky to plan the funeral and to help Dad. That was the first funeral I had planned, and I learned how some funeral directors trade on your grief and try to get you to pay as much as possible.

In September, we were transferred back to Houston, where Jenks was named General Manager of Marketing. After a few years, Jenks had the job of his dreams—Vice President of World-Wide Marketing. Before moving into our new house on St. Mary's Lane, Jenks and I drove Toby to college. Since our home was not yet finished, we left the kids at the motel with Rick in charge for the day.

Neither Rick nor Susan was happy about moving to Houston. Rick was a senior and because of strict eligibility rules for athletes, he could not play football or any sport for a year. He made a wonderful adjustment and decided to make all A's during his senior year. Both Susan and Rick missed their friends, so at Thanksgiving, we sent them back to Kansas City on the train for a visit. Rick and Susan did not always get along so I had to impress on Rick that he was "the big brother" and was in charge of keeping Suzi safe and happy. I sent them off with lots of ham sandwiches and treats. They had a good trip, but neither wanted to move back to Kansas.

After graduating from high school, Rick's goal was to earn enough money to buy a car. Not just any car. He found an ad for an old Jaguar and asked Jenks to go with him to look at it. I reminded Jenks that his job was to keep Rick from buying this expensive car.

When they got home, Jenks told me, "Rick just bought the cutest little car you have ever seen."

Rick did drive off to college in his Jag and was really

pleased with himself. Of course, it was a problem as long as he had it.

Toby was hired to be a member of the College Board at Neiman-Marcus during the summer. One day she went across the street to get a sandwich. An older man came to her table and said, "I see you at Neiman-Marcus. May I join you for lunch?"

She agreed and he asked, "What do you do at the store?" After she told him, Toby asked, "What do you do?"

He responded, "Oh, I do a lot of things. I am Stanley Marcus."

Toby married Bill Howard in 1971.

A few years later, Susan joined Rick at the University of Texas. During winter vacation, Rick went to Alaska to work on an oil rig in Prudhoe Bay. He left the Jag at home for me to try to sell. He gave me a driving lesson, thinking I did not know how to shift gears. I told him I learned to drive with a stick shift when I was 14.

After Bob graduated from high school in 1973, he organized his football buddies into a painting company and made enough money painting houses to buy a used Volvo. Bob drove himself to California, where he attended Stanford University.

With all the kids gone, I was ready for my next career—something more challenging than playing tennis with other empty nesters. I applied to go to graduate school at the University of Houston and was rejected. At 52 I was considered too old. I was disappointed. Then I got angry and called for an appointment to talk to the admissions counselor. The receptionist told me they don't usually give appointments. I replied, "People my age don't usually apply."

The admissions person agreed to see me. I was nervous. My hands were sweating. He asked, "Mrs. Jenkins, why would you want to go back to school at your age? It has been 30 years since you graduated from college. We have to save places in grad school for people we think can make a difference. At your age do you think that is possible? Do you think you could keep up with younger students?"

I answered the best I could, and he replied, "We want to save places for minority students." I reminded him, "Sir, I am an older woman. I would be a minority student." He almost smiled and said, "Well, Mrs. Jenkins, this next class does need a psychologically mature white female, and you might fit the bill."

I was accepted as their token little old white lady.

While I waited to begin graduate school, I signed up for a course to see if I really could handle college after 30 years. The only class open was Human Sexuality. Since I was married with kids, I thought I knew enough to pass a course in sex education. But I was almost wrong.

The professor was a popular teacher, and there were 999 young college kids in the auditorium and me—a psychologically mature little old white lady. The teacher brought in speakers to talk to the class about their lifestyles—relationships I knew nothing about. We heard from gay couples, prostitutes, lesbian women, cross-dressers and transgender people. Also, there was a lecture on group sex.

In the middle of one class, seven men dressed only in hats, belts and sneakers ran across the stage, jumped down beside me, sitting on the aisle seat in the first row, and ran out the back door.

The teacher asked if anyone was offended. I raised my hand. A student with a microphone rushed up to me to give my answer. The professor asked, "What offended you?" I said, "There were no women represented."

The auditorium erupted into shouts, foot-stomping, clapping and cheers. The teacher asked, "Would you be willing to organize your own demonstration of women for extra credit?" I turned down that opportunity, but I made an A in the course. I wrote our daughter, Susan, in college to tell her I made an A in sex. She sent me a dollar.

Graduate school was difficult. I was older than my classmates, teachers, the dean and the president. While I dressed in my Neiman-Marcus slacks, boots and sweater, most students came to class in shorts, flip-flops and T-shirts that said something like, "Authority sucks." In 30 years, the dress code on campus had changed dramatically.

On the first day of graduate school in the fall, the teacher asked each one of us to stand and introduce ourselves. When it was my turn, I said, "I am Margie Jenkins, married for 27 years, mother of four kids. I have been a teacher, volunteer at my church and a room mother at schools. I am looking forward to being certified as a person beyond being a wife and mother."

A big African-American man stood up in the back row and said, "We don't need people like you in this class. Why don't you go home to your fancy family and your husband who probably works for some obnoxious oil company? We have screwed around with this introduction shit long enough. Let's get on with the program."

No one said a word except the young woman from Hong Kong sitting next to me. She leaned over and asked in her halting English, "What does 'screw around with shit' mean?"

One day, I was relieved to see a bulletin board announcement: "GAA meeting tonight—Everyone welcome." In high school and college, I had been active in the Girls Athletic Association. It would be great to be involved with other girls who enjoyed physical activities. While I studied the bulletin board, two girls came up behind me, slapped me on the butt and said, "Hey, you interested in that group?"

"I might be," I answered. "It's been a long time since I was active in GAA, but I think I would enjoy it." With another slap on my butt, they called out, "See you tonight." And they left.

While standing there, another group of girls asked me, "Are you going to that meeting of the Gay Alliance Association?" I changed my mind.

Chester was a young man with a squeaky voice who was in many of my classes. He had long, straggly hair, earrings, Coke bottle glasses, and he often came to school barefoot. I tried to avoid him. In one class we had to do some kind of computer stuff. At that time there were no personal computers, but the university had a huge computer in a special room. Each student had to insert a card containing his or her information into the computer to get results. I spent long hours in that room trying to get my cards to come out with the right answers. It wasn't happening.

One day as I sat in that room waiting again for my computer card to come out right, Chester walked into the room. He smiled at me and asked in his squeaky voice, "How are you doing?"

I said, "I give up. I can't get this thing to work for me."

Chester said, "Let me try." He inserted my card in the huge machine, pushed different buttons and it came out perfect.

He and I sat in the computer room and visited. He said he was gay, a vegetarian and loved all kinds of electronics. "My father works for Exxon, and he only cares about moving our family all over the world and making a pile of money. That's not my bag. I'm going to do something different."

I thanked him for helping me and left. The next day, I took a bag of Texas red grapefruit for him and his partner to enjoy.

After two years, on graduation day, our group met in a special room. A nice-looking guy wearing a dark blue suit and shiny new shoes walked up to me. When he spoke in his squeaky voice, I recognized Chester with a fresh new haircut and contact lenses. I greeted him, and he picked me up and swung me around in a circle and kissed my forehead.

"Margie," he said, "You have been my best friend these two years. I really appreciate you."

I said, "Chester, you look wonderful."

He smiled and said, "Today I have an interview with a great agency. I hope to make a good impression and earn a lot of money."

I hugged him and said, "Chester, you will make a great impression. Good luck to you."

In 1976, Toby had Amanda, our first grandchild. Three years later, Toby was a single mother. Her husband divorced her to marry his secretary. Toby traveled for

Jones of New York for several years and then became a public relations person before she married Joe Gilbert. They were married for 20 years before he died.

Susan married Ken Bean in the chapel of our church and a few years later in 1979, they had our first and only grandson, John. They divorced when John was 5. Susan went to law school and became an attorney in Raleigh, North Carolina.

After graduation, I had just started working at my church and was in the middle of a therapy session when the church secretary knocked on my door to say, "There is a long-distance phone call for you." I did not usually get phone calls at work.

I excused myself and went to the office to answer the phone.

A male voice said, "Hi, Mom, I just got married."

"OK," I said, "but which son is this?"

He answered, "Hey, Mom, it's Rick. Dede and I just got married. We're heading out for our honeymoon in St. Maarten Island in the West Indies."

"Congratulations to you both," I said, and we hung up.

Rick and Dede have now been married over 40 years and have had a successful real estate company during that time.

I became a counselor at Interface Counseling Center, and in 1981 I opened my own private practice.

In 1982, Bob married Nancy Wheeler, whom he had met at Stanford. They were married in the apple orchard of her parents' home. Bob asked me to be his "best man," which was a special experience. We played tennis with the bride and groom in the morning, and they married in the afternoon. Later, they had two daughters, Kacie and Brodie. Today they live in Sebastopol, California, where Bob has a small vineyard.

A lot of clients I was seeing in my office were facing end-of-life issues. I saw a need for workshops on preparing for life's last adventure. I published two books on the subject, *You Only Die Once*, and a companion workbook, *My Personal Planner*.

In 1984 Jenks retired from Conoco after nearly 35 years, and Rick asked him to become his partner in a new company called Austin Custom Homes. Jenks spent most weeks in Austin but came home on weekends. He and Rick enjoyed working together, and it was a great adventure for both of them. After several years, Jenks felt Rick was doing most of the work and made a decision to have Rick take over the whole company. Jenks began playing tennis with a group of guys, and that was a nice change for him.

In May 1984 Jenks and I went to Kentucky to plan a 100th birthday party for my dad, who was living in Carmel Manor nursing home. The nuns invited our family to stay at their guest cottage, and we had a fantastic celebration. Afterwards, Dad took my hand and said, "Margie, you and Jenks made a great celebration for me. You seem to be able to do everything. I am 100 years old. I can't hear. I don't see very well, I hurt all over. I have lived long enough. I have had a great life. I want you to help me die. When our animals got to the point where they could not enjoy life, we let them die."

I said, "God is not ready for you yet. We have to go to Plan B."

In October, Sister Rose called to say Dad was not doing well, maybe we should come home. I told her we were planning to leave for Greece the next day, but I would cancel our trip if Dad wanted me to come to Kentucky right away.

Sister Rose explained the situation to my dad, then put him on the phone. I knew he couldn't hear me but I could hear him.

In a hoarse voice, Dad said, "You and Jenks go to Greece, bring me some Greek cigars, God go with you, have a good time. I will be here when you get back."

We went to Greece the next day and had a great time. When we got home, I called Sister Rose and said, "We are home. We brought Dad some Greek cigars, and we will be in Kentucky tomorrow." She gave Dad the message.

Dad repeated what he heard Sister Rose say: "Margie and Jenks are home from Greece. They had a good time. They brought me some Greek cigars. That's good."

And he died.

At least he waited until we got home.

When we got to Carmel Manor the next day, I discovered an envelope on his desk in his room. He had written out instructions for his memorial service. "Have the nuns play their guitars and sing, and you and Jenks lead the service. Love, Dad."

All our kids and their families came to Dad's service. Most of the nuns and residents of Carmel Manor attended. It was a great celebration of Dad's life.

In 2002, I became the CEO of my own company, Patio Press. Jenks and I traveled all over the country talking about my books and the benefits of preparing for life's ending. We spoke at churches, retirement communities, universities, book clubs, social work conferences, and aging agencies. We had a great time, met wonderful friends and felt we made a difference in people's lives.

After 35 years as a psychotherapist in Houston, I retired at age 91. With Jenks' help, we created a video course called *You Only Die Once*.

Several years ago, when Jenks and I were relaxing on the back patio with a glass of wine, cheese and crackers, Jenks took my hand and said, "Margie, can you believe what a fabulous life we have had together? Almost 70 years. We helped each other have successful careers, and we raised four great kids. You did most of the parenting, and I am very proud of our family. You were a fantastic mother. I wish I had been a better parent. You supported me the first 30 years of our marriage. I supported you in the next 30 years of our marriage. Now we can just relax, sit back and enjoy our successes and our family. We have had a magical life together. Thank you for making it so special."

He kissed me.

Chapter 10

LIFE WITHOUT JENKS

Jenks was part of my life for almost 80 years, beginning in 1938 when we met in Newport High School. I fondly remember our first bediddle kiss.

Our eight-year courtship was rocky at times, but I never gave up. We both agreed that our 70 years of marriage were magical. Of course, it was not perfect—but we made it work until the end.

On March 22, 2016, we dressed to work out at the gym. We were both 93. After completing some computer work I called to Jenks that I was ready to go.

"First, I'll make a pit stop," he said.

Flor, our special housekeeper, was going to the gym with us. She noticed Jenks was in the bathroom longer than usual. She called to him, "Mr. Jenks are you OK?"

He replied, "No, I am not."

Flor signaled to me that something was wrong, and I followed her into the bathroom. Jenks was sitting on the toilet, his hands on his stomach. Flor put a cool cloth on his forehead and kissed the top of his head. I kneeled down in front of him and grabbed his hands.

"Jenks, what are you feeling?" I asked.

He looked at me and said, "I don't feel right. It is hard to breathe. My stomach feels weird."

Flor asked, "Mr. Jenks, should we call the hospice nurse?" He said yes; he must have known this was not an ordinary stomachache.

Paige came as soon as I called. After checking him in the bathroom, she nodded to me and said, "Mr. Jenks is failing."

I kissed him and said, "Hey Jenks, we always agreed we'd like to die at home, but you don't have to die on the toilet."

He smiled.

I said, "I love you, Jenks."

He squeezed my hands and said, "I love you, Margie."

I watched as his eyes rolled up in his head and his body went limp.

Flor and I hugged him. She said, "That all happened in 20 minutes."

"That's called a good death," I said. "He knew he was loved and died peacefully."

Jenks died just four days after signing up for hospice. We had invited their staff to come and talk to us and our daughters about the benefits. Since Jenks had had a stroke one year before, the hospice nurse suggested Jenks sign up now. That was Friday, March 18. He died the following Tuesday.

On the day Jenks died, Paige called 911, and the firefighters and emergency medical technicians came immediately. They moved Jenks from the toilet to our bed. Flor gently closed his eyes, covered him with a quilt and shut the door behind her. I removed his wedding ring and watch. They were still warm in the palm of my hand. I stretched out next to him, put my arms around him and kissed his face. Tears filled my eyes. I thanked God for our long life together. I prayed, "God, take Jenks from my arms to yours."

I invited Toby, Susan, and Flor to come into the bedroom

with me. Flor prayed and thanked God for Jenks, his good humor and his loving spirit. I said, "I have no regrets. We had a great life together. He had a good death."

Toby said, "Mom, it is amazing that you can say that."

I called Rick and Bob. They came right away. While Flor, the girls and I were saying our goodbyes to Jenks, hospice called Claire Brothers Funeral Home. Their staff came, covered Jenks with a maroon blanket and rolled him out of the house. It was difficult to let him go. A part of me went out the door with him.

We planned Jenks' memorial service for May when all the family could attend. Susan made a video of Jenks' life to show at the reception. The other three kids and I spoke at the service, remembering the good times of our lives with Jenks.

Since we had co-authored two books on preparing for life's ending—and given over 100 presentations on the subject—we were as prepared as we could be for death. Still, I felt a part of me had died. I had a hole in my heart. Although family and friends were supportive, I alone had to deal with my grief. It was hard to sleep alone in our big bed. I suffered arterial fibrillation—A-Fib. My heart raced. I couldn't eat. Some nights I couldn't breathe and thought I was having a heart attack. Our daughters took me to the emergency room. But the problem was extreme grief. The world was a different shape without Jenks.

I tried to act normal but there was no normal.

Several weeks after Jenks died, I went to La Madeleine Café just like Jenks and I used to do and had an apple turnover. I sat in the sunshine and thanked God that he let Jenks die first so he did not have to live alone.

He had often said to me, "Remember, Margie, I have dibs on dying first. My life wouldn't work without you."

About a month before Jenks died, we were sitting in the den watching TV, holding hands, when he looked at me and said, "Margie we have had an amazing life together. We created a great family. We traveled the world and visited all seven continents, including the Antarctic. If we lived another 50 years, you would no doubt make reservations for us to go to the moon. You planned most of our vacations, and I often wondered why we were exploring the Antarctic or visiting Vietnam or roaming along the silk route of southern Russia, but they were all special experiences.

"In one Russian village, we saw two little old peasant men. You figured out a way to sit with them on the curb and have your picture taken. You put your hand on their knees, and they smiled. We have that picture. Later, we were told 'women do not touch men.' Leave it to you, Margie, to go against the rules."

After a long silence, Jenks said, "You know, if I died tonight, it would be OK. I have had a great life. Our marriage surpassed my wildest dreams."

Jenks once said that when he died, he wanted to come back as a great blue heron like those that visit our yard. They are so spectacular with their huge wingspan.

The day Jenks died, a beautiful blue heron landed in the garden. I knew it was Jenks coming to say he was OK, and I would be OK, too.

Living alone was a new experience. Everything changed. One less plate on the table. No one sleeping on the other side of my bed. Driving the car with no passenger beside me. In church, when we sang one of Jenks' favorite hymns, I turned to him, but he was not there. Watching families of baby ducks in our lake lost a lot of its intrigue without Jenks. Going to the gym by myself was a lonely experience. When anyone talked to me about Jenks, I cried. Would I ever get used to being without him?

One day at La Madeleine, I saw an older couple sitting out on the patio, holding hands and sharing a piece of coconut cake. Although tears came to my eyes remembering we did that, too, it was a good reminder that love goes on.

Toby and Susan constantly check on me. They invite me to accompany them to various events. They are loving and supportive and allow me to cry without embarrassment. We even enjoy moments of laughter.

Getting the car repaired, calling a plumber to fix the water leak, renewing insurance—all tasks that Jenks did. Will life ever feel normal again?

Bob invited me to California to spend a week in July. Traveling alone felt weird, but I did it. My time with Bob and Nancy was healing. When I got home, accepting lunch invitations from friends seemed easier.

Rick and Dede check on me often and come to visit.

As the months and years have gone by, I have become more comfortable being by myself. But once in a while, unexpectedly, the tears come.

People handle grief differently. Some stay in bed. Others drown their sadness with drink or drugs. Some try to hide their grief. Others do busy work and don't take time to grieve. I believe it is important to accept the grief, feel the feelings and let the tears fall.

Otherwise, recovery is only delayed.

For me, writing about my loss has been healing. Writing letters to Jenks has been helpful.

In a file I keep of "love letters from Jenks," I found this birthday greeting when I was 74:

"TO MARGIE, THE BIRTHDAY GIRL ON MAY 28, 1997"

"What a fortunate happening—my picking you and you picking me. The stars were in special alignment, and the journey for a lifetime was launched. Full of fun, laughter, travel around the world, great family, surprises and successes."

"You are the most outstanding person I know. A mountain of strength and tenderness. A person of talent and achievement that most only dream about."

"What does all this add up to—well, for me a giant 'whoopee' and a big thank you for loving me. I love you, Margie. Congratulations on a life well spent. Love, Jenks"

It is now over three years since Jenks died and I still miss him greatly—his smile, his presence and his upbeat attitude about life.

One of my rules for enjoying life to the fullest has always been to have a purpose and a schedule. Without Jenks, I lost my purpose, life lost its sparkle. I struggle to schedule an outing each day that gets me out of the house. I want to reconnect with friends, keep my mind active by writing about Jenks and make a schedule to go back to the gym. I focus on finding something each day for which I am grateful. Family and friends give me many reasons to be thankful.

I thank God for challenges in life and ask for guidance to make the best decisions. Forgiving is healing, and forgiving myself is most difficult. I made mistakes in our marriage and in parenting our kids. But in most cases, I did the best I could. I made a rule that I try to follow—if I can do something to fix what's wrong, I do the best I can. If I can't do anything about it, I give it to God. God has a lot of my stuff.

My life goal has always been to see the good in others, keep a sense of humor and be kind to myself. And I try never to forget – love is the answer.

I want to continue to have a purpose and a schedule, share love and forgiveness along the way and live bodaciously as long as I can.

Made in the USA
Las Vegas, NV
16 February 2022